PEACE *or* PERISH

There is No Other Choice

Stepping Stones for Turbulent Times

J.P. Vaswani

Other Titles by J.P. Vaswani

NEW YOU BOOKS

PEACE *or* PERISH
There is No Other Choice

Stepping Stones for Turbulent Times

J.P. Vaswani

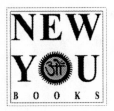

New You Books is an imprint of Sadhu Vaswani Center, USA
www.newyoubooks.com
www.sadhuvaswani.org

Bloomington, IN Milton Keynes, UK

AuthorHouse™
1663 Liberty Drive, Suite 200
Bloomington, IN 47403
www.authorhouse.com
Phone: 1-800-839-8640

AuthorHouse™ UK Ltd.
500 Avebury Boulevard
Central Milton Keynes, MK9 2BE
www.authorhouse.co.uk
Phone: 08001974150

First published by AuthorHouse 3/21/2007
ISBN: 978-1-4343-0371-4 (sc)
ISBN: 978-1-4343-0372-1 (hc)

Printed in the United States of America
Bloomington, Indiana
This book is printed on acid-free paper.

New You Books
94 Durie Avenue
Closter, NJ 07064

www.newyoubooks.com
www.sadhuvaswani.org

To my Guru and Guide,
Master and Mentor
SADHU VASWANI
An Apostle of Peace and Non-violence
A Picture of Love and Compassion,
Of Simplicity and Service,
Of Self-effacement and Sacrifice-
I give back to you what already belongs to you.
                                    J.P. Vaswani

To a high military official who asked for advice,
Sadhu Vaswani said:
"Love peace in the heart within but
Keep the powder dry!"

Contents

Foreword

"Since wars begin in the minds of men, it is in the minds of men that the defenses of peace must be constructed." ... So begins the Constitution of the United Nations Educational, Scientific and Cultural Organization (UNESCO). And it goes on to acknowledge, quite openly, that a peace that is based exclusively on economic or political arrangements among governments will not last – that individual people must also find common ground if we are to build the kind of world we all aspire to.

And it is to the minds of men and women that Dada J.P. Vaswani appeals. He seeks to inspire us by posing bare-faced the kind of questions that often lay buried beneath the surfaces of our busy lives—philosophers' questions, about why we are as we are, and about what it is in life itself that helps or hinders us as we strive for peace and happiness and contentment. And he offers his insights in language that any sincere seeker will be able to follow.

I have spent a great deal of my professional life urging governments to work together to achieve the very political and economic agreements that underpin a better world. And I am convinced that these agreements are essential for world peace. But I know—like the drafters of the UNESCO Constitution knew—that even though they are essential, they are not sufficient. Dada's book, *Peace or Perish: There is No Other Choice* challenges us to take up the complements to diplomacy and governance. It is a challenge that is no less difficult than the challenges the UN faces, and one that is also no less important. It is the challenge to change ourselves.

Shashi Tharoor
Under-Secretary-General for Communications and Public Information to the United Nations
February 20, 2007

Preface

How can there be peace on earth when
the hearts of men are a volcano?
—Sadhu Vaswani

There once was a king who commissioned the best artists in his kingdom to paint a picture that would reflect the very essence of peace. Hundreds of pictures were brought for the royal view: artists had imaginatively represented peace in all shapes, forms and images— vast open spaces, blue skies, calm and deep blue seas, uninhabited planes, snow—capped mountain peaks, the wide—open eyes of a little child.

Of all the pictures, the king chose one which captured his imagination. His courtiers crowded all around to see the picture, and they stared at each other in perplexity. How could *this* be the king's idea of peace?

The picture was of a huge and turbulent waterfall. The roaring waters thundered down from a great height—you could almost hear the roar, you could almost sense the height. The waters fell on a rocky surface and splashed everywhere. A cloud of spray arose over the falls and a huge lake—nay, a sea of water seemed to stretch below.

"Excuse me, your majesty," said the boldest among the courtiers. "This is indeed an awesome sight, for the head reels to see the huge waterfall in all its force and fury. But how can this picture possibly represent *peace*?"

The king smiled. "Look carefully at the picture," he said to them. "Is there nothing else you can see?"

The courtiers looked as carefully as they could. And yet they could see nothing to suggest peace in the picture of the mighty, roaring waterfall.

The king drew their attention to the bare rock wall against which the water was falling. In a small, deep niche within the rock was a secure, cozy nest. In the nest, the mother-bird was feeding her babies—cute little fledglings, who eagerly looked up at her with open mouths, their beady eyes and upturned beaks the very symbols of hope, trust and faith. The roar of the water was just a few feet away—but the birds were in a world apart—a world of their own peaceful making! They were at peace with themselves, at peace with their surroundings.

Peace prevailed in their little world—unaffected by the thunderous roar of the outer world.

Peace may be fragile and vulnerable—but peace is possible, and peace is attainable, even in a turbulent world like ours.

I
THE CHALLENGES OF LIFE

The Million Dollar Question

If someone were to ask you, "What does life mean to you?" When asked this question, most of us close our eyes for a brief moment and plunge into thought. We are unable to answer right away; and after a vague random sentence or two, we honestly reply with a sigh, "Actually, I don't know."

Philosophers and thinkers have given us thousands of 'definitions' in answer to this question. There is one that comes to my mind right away: "To the man who believes that life is worth living—life becomes worth living."

Life means something different to different people; happy people will view life very differently from unhappy people.

By the same token, busy, active, working people will view life differently from reflective, contemplative, or meditative people.

Many people think that life is meant to be lived for *others*; while some are apt to imagine that life must be lived on *their own terms*.

Is life then all about being useful—making every moment worthwhile?

Some people try to come to terms with life through their intellect. "I think, therefore I am," they insist, using the Cartesian principle. Life, to them, is a problem that must be grappled with through reason.

For some, life is an enigma, a painful mystery. But as they grapple with pain and suffering, even they come to realize that though life may seem cruel and unfair, it actually works.

Sometimes it's the *difference* between them and others that bothers people a great deal. They tend to look at life through their own narrow viewpoint—and think that all others are crazy and insane, because they don't share those views.

Some of us are horrified by the hatred and the violence around us. Rashly, we jump to the conclusion that life is meaningless.

Life's but a walking shadow,
A poor player that struts and frets his hour upon the stage
And then is heard no more: it is a tale told by an idiot,
Full of sound and fury,
Signifying nothing.

—Shakespeare

The power and the imagination of the above lines of poetry are so effective that we are apt to conclude that this is indeed Shakespeare's "philosophy of life".

Nothing could be further from the truth. These lines were uttered by the tragic hero Macbeth, who had chosen the palm of evil to accomplish something, which he thought would be noble, worthwhile and grand, only to discover to his horror that he only faced an abyss of emptiness. In context, these lines bring out the dissolution of a man who has sadly misunderstood the meaning of life. The unfortunate thing is that these lines are often quoted out of context to justify a cynical, negative, nihilistic view of life.

There are at least hundred such 'definitions' I have come across. And they remind me of Samuel Butler's words: "Life is the art of drawing sufficient conclusions from insufficient premises."

If you thought that those lines from Shakespeare's *Macbeth* were a bit heavy for you, here is a light-hearted collection that is often quoted:

Life is a battle—fight it.
Life is an adventure—explore it.
Life is a lesson—learn it.
Life is a garden—cultivate it.
Life is a mission—fulfill it.
Life is a journey—follow it.
Life is a roller coaster—take its ups and downs.
Life is a prison—there's no escape.

We are born here on earth—and life is to be lived in a fitting way. Therefore life is too valuable to be summarized or defined so lightly and abruptly. Wouldn't you agree?

Let us begin the search, the discovery of the right way to understand life which in all ways is itself a challenge.

Life is a Challenge...
Life Seems Unfair...

In Dostoevsky's masterpiece, *The Brothers Karamazov*, there is a heated discussion about religion, God, and justice in Book Five. One of the debaters gives us a graphic account of the sufferings experienced by abuse and tortured children in Russia. He questions how any merciful, supernatural power could permit such atrocities to occur under His dispensation.

You do not have to read Dostoevsky to become aware of the atrocities that are happening all over the world. You don't even have to switch on your TV to watch news broadcasts, which are full of such violence; you don't even have to turn the pages of the newspaper to keep track of what's happening. The people you meet at work, the commuters who travel with you, even the stranger you meet on the street, everyone is talking about the latest act of violence—until a new horror pushes it aside.

Millions of viewers watch atrocities live nowadays—buildings, cities being bombed; planes hijacked; subway stations and trains targeted; and innocent lives ruthlessly destroyed.

On July 11, 2006, suburban local trains in Mumbai were subject to a series of bomb—blasts during the peak hours. Hundreds upon hundreds of innocent civilians perished in the disaster. Old men, returning home after transacting some business in the city; fathers and husbands who were the mainstay and support of their families as the sole earning members; young men full of hopes and dreams for a bright future; affluent, well—to—do traders as well as honest, hardworking clerks; doctors, engineers, accountants, stock brokers, shopkeepers, accountants and even social workers—all were killed for no rhyme or reason.

Why?

Life is a Challenge...
Life Seems So Tragic ...

I was told of a learned scientist, a senior government servant who headed one of the country's premier research institutions. An honest, upright, efficient administrator, he had reached the top of his career ladder, and was looking forward to a peaceful, contented retirement. Three years before he was due to retire, he lost his beloved wife.

The effect on this amicable, respected, senior scientist was devastating. He shut himself away in his home and refused to meet people, or even face the world outside. A close friend who went to visit him a month after the tragedy, was shocked to see his condition—indeed, the state of his house, and the utter misery in which he lived.

Some years ago, in the Indian city of Pune, an auto rickshaw ferrying children to school met with an accident and five little kids, aged between 6 and 9 were killed in the mishap. The whole city was shocked by the tragic loss and mourned with the inconsolable parents, who were devastated by the sudden blow.

How do people cope with personal tragedies like this?

What seems to be even more cruel and futile is the growing number of young students who seek to end their own life—just because they didn't score high marks or because they failed to get into the course of their choice. A promising life is nipped off in the bud, and parents are left with a double loss—the death of their loving child, and the manner in which the child put an end to his/her life, when the parents were close at hand to offer every support they could possibly give.

Why?

Life is a Challenge...
Life Seems So Unjust...

Statistics proclaim that there are more millionaires in the world, than ever before. We no longer talk about very rich people; we now talk about HNWI—High Net Worth Individuals, whose disposable income and spending power are increasing phenomenally. I am told that living within your means is no longer fashionable; saving and planning for the future are passé; instead, the *mantra* is: spend, Spend, SPEND!

Unfortunately, it is not only people's spending power that has grown; pove· · is growing too, side by side. And if HNWI's are on t rise, people classified as BPL— Below the Poverty Line – are also multiplying.

The result is that the gap between the haves and have-nots has widened, and everywhere in the world, the rich are getting richer and the poor are getting poorer. While economists and bankers are talking about 'growth' and booming economies, people are still dying of malnutrition and avoidable diseases!

Sometime ago, we heard the heart-rending story of a poor family in North India, who appealed to the President, to obtain legal sanction for the euthanasia of their teenage son who was suffering from an acutely painful disease for which they could not afford treatment; and for which the local government hospitals could not (or would not) offer them even palliative care.

Consider the tremendous progress we have made in advanced medical care. Consider too that people now live much longer than their ancestors did. Consider the miracles and marvels of modern medicine—the life-saving drugs and surgical treatments now available to us. How can we reconcile this with the painful fact that even basic healthcare is not available to the less fortunate. When a citizen of a democratic republic appeals to the authorities for the right to take away his child's life, are we not likely to wonder if we are living in a civilized society? Where lies hidden the conscience of the nation? What is the purpose served by the elected government? What is the world coming to?

"Justice delayed is justice denied," goes the saying. Alas, speedy justice is available only for the rich, the powerful; the bold and the beautiful, as they are called. As for the poor, the wretched, the landless and powerless, the law is a dark room in which blind justice languishes. Time and again we hear of rich and influential men committing atrocities and crimes—and getting away scot-free!

Where is justice?

Life is a Challenge...
Life Seems So Insecure...

For millions of ordinary men and women all over the world, life continues to be a struggle for survival.

On the garbage dumps of Sao Paulo, Chennai and Dhaka, men, women and children forage for subsistence. In war-torn, famine-stricken Northern African nations, people face starvation and utter poverty. If the numbers of educated unemployed youth keeps swelling in Western countries, they have the dole to fall back on; in the developing world, no such hand-outs are available.

It is not as if those who are employed are feeling secure; the 'pink slip' is a permanent cause for fear and anxiety. Recession, competition and the ever-present threat of closure are causing thousands of workers to fear for their livelihood.

A peaceful retirement is now a pipe-dream for the ordinary worker. Inflation and rising prices mean that his pension will never keep up with the cost of living, as he grows older. Thus there is fear and insecurity about growing older. "Who will pay my medical bills? Who will provide hospitalization? How will I make ends meet? What will happen to me in my old age?"

A friend read out an excerpt from a news feature to me the other day. A reputed psychiatrist is quoted as saying: "We are moving from a repair economy to a replacement one—whether it's a car or a washing machine, or even a spouse!" So much for the security and sanctity of the institution of marriage!

How should we feel secure in this insecure world?

Whither Human Rights?

An Antarctic explorer was asked to identify the most difficult ordeal he faced on his expedition to the South Pole. After a moment's thought he said, "It is when you cross four or five miles of snow and ice in twelve hours—and then realize that due to the drifting of the ice—cap, you have lost three miles of territory in the process. I tell you, this is really disheartening!"

Current civilization faces similar crisis. We proclaim loudly of our 'progress', 'development' and 'advancement'. But all around us, civilization seems to be regressing towards the dark ages! Man's inhumanity to man has exceeded all conceivable limits today. Starting with atrocities of the holocaust, the inhumane treatment of prisoners of war and the ultimate horror of the H-Bomb dropped on Hiroshima and Nagasaki, the Second

World War revealed the depths to which our wounded civilization could sink.

Since then, the horrors have continued unabated. Mass-murderers and aggressors call themselves freedom-fighters; violence and bloodshed are justified in the name of religion; and governments stoop so low as to indulge in the genocide of their own people.

What is happening to human rights?

Life is a Challenge…
Life is Full of Prejudices…

Modern scholars call it fear of 'the other'—prejudice against, even hatred of people who are *not like us*—people with a different color of skin, people speaking a different language, people professing a different faith are not to be trusted; worse, they are actively targeted and vilified.

We talk of the world shrinking and becoming a global village; indeed, all of us are only too eager to buy and sell, do business with all corners, but underneath, deep distrust and prejudice prevails.

Colonization may be a thing of the past, but economic and political hegemony prevails in other and more subtle forms.

'Foreigners' are treated with suspicion—especially those belonging to 'other' races and religions.

Strangers who talk differently and dress differently are subject to being treated as criminals or terrorists. If you don't like the look of your fellow-passenger on a flight, you can actually 'offload' him like a piece of luggage.

And we are used to speak in glowing terms about something called, 'The Brotherhood of Man!'

Where is Humanity?

Life is a Challenge...
Life Seems So Heartless...

Shakespeare's *King Lear* dramatizes the tragedy of a king, an old man, father of three grown—up daughters, who decides to divide his kingdom among them so that he may live the autumn of his life free from cares and worldly responsibilities. Unfortunately, he disinherits one of them, his favorite daughter, because she refuses to flatter his ego by telling him how much she loves him. His kingdom is given to the two other elder daughters. No sooner do they inherit his power and his wealth, than they begin to reveal their true colors. The old father is insulted, abused and finally turned out of doors on a stormy night to brave the elements. Unable to comprehend, leave alone come to terms with such blatant ingratitude, the old king loses his sanity.

What would you say—a familiar story these days?

"Every old man is also a King Lear," said Goethe, the German writer. Indeed, old age homes in 21st century India, are full of old men and women who have not only given the best years of their life to their children—but also bestowed their life-savings, pensions and provident fund to their offspring in the fond hope that they will be loved and cared for in their old age—only to be 'dumped' in such homes when the children no longer need them!

I do not exaggerate. A distinguished social worker from Chennai, who has dedicated her life to caring for such destitute senior citizens, remarked that old mothers and fathers are literally driven out of their homes when they are no longer 'useful'—when the mother is too old to cook and clean and take care of the house, and the father is too ill or senile to fetch rations and pay utility bills and walk the children to school and back.

That is not all. She also says that when these 'orphaned' old people die in the old age homes, their sons and daughters do not bother to arrange for their last rites, or even attend the funerals arranged by the volunteers serving in the homes. Some of them send a little money to cover funeral expenses. Others simply express their inability to come and tell the volunteers to do whatever they think fit!

No, this is not fiction. It is reality. In a particular lawsuit filed by destitute parents, the court has actually ordered the sons to look after their parents or pay a certain amount to them for their upkeep.

The fundamental values of our society are being eroded with the fragmentation of families and the rejection of old people—and 'unwanted' children. For, at the other end of the spectrum, our orphanages are also overflowing with abandoned children—especially girl children, who, it seems, are really children of a lesser god! Why else would their own mothers abandon them on rubbish heaps and street corners?

Do our hearts beat within us? Are we human beings with a heart, mind and soul?

Life is a Challenge...
What about Religion?

Today, man is losing faith in religion, because religion has been separated from life. Quarrels, discord, hatred and strife have entered the sphere of religion. Sad to say, religion, which was meant to be a bond of union, has become a source of sectarian strife and violence.

In the name of secularism, we are making the tragic mistake of discarding religion from our lives. We have 'sanitized' our schools and colleges by keeping God out of education. How can such education work?

Today, religion is discredited by 'liberals' and 'intellectuals'. I would like to say to them: It is not religion that has failed us; it is we who have failed religion. We talk of religion a great deal; but we do not bear witness to religion in deeds of daily living. We pay no heed to the teachings of the great saints and prophets of humanity.

It is life that is needed—not words. I may go to the church, to the mosque, to the temple everyday. I may chant hymns and sing songs of praise. I may read unending passages from the scriptures. I may fast from dawn to dusk—but if my life does not bear witness to the great ideals of my faith in deeds of daily life, I am no better than a tape-recorder!

I may deliver inspiring sermons; I may write learned commentaries on the Gita, the Upanishads, the Brahma Sutras or other scriptures—but if my life does not reflect their great truths in deeds of daily life, I am no better than a printing machine!

Today, the world does not want tape-recorders or printing machines. Life is needed, not words. Action is needed, not rituals. Religion needs to be re-interpreted in terms of energy, vitality, life.

In a world torn by sectarianism and intolerance, religion is exploited by unscrupulous elements that fan the flames of hatred in the name of their faith and belief. At the same time, it has become habitual for politicians to blame religion for all the evils of society. Thus religion today has been made a scapegoat for all the atrocities perpetrated by man. Terrorism, bloodshed and the killing of innocent men and women are all labeled as 'religious' strife.

Religion came to unite, reconcile, to create harmony among men.

Dharam to hai pyaar
Dharam to hai muhobbat
Dharam to hai prem
Dharam to hai sulah
Dharam to hai shanti
Dharam to hai seva.

Religion is love
Religion is pure affection
Religion is peace
Religion is service!

If we believe the above to be true, how can brother kill brother, how can one human being torture his fellow man in the name of religion?

Life is a Challenge...
and Peace Eludes Us...

A few years ago, the *International Review of Diplomatic Studies* published in Geneva, calculated the cost of World War II, in the following terms:

* 22 million men—killed in action
* 29 million men—wounded, mutilated on incapacitated
* 21 million people—evacuated, deported or displaced
* 39 million homes—reduced to ashes / rubble
* 150 million people—rendered homeless

Up until 1946, the war cost enough to provide the following—let me rephrase that—the expenses incurred by the war *could have* been used to provide the following facilities to every family in U.S.A., Canada, Austria, Britain, France, the U.S.S.R., Germany, and Belgium.

* A home costing $18,000
* Furniture worth $ 6,000
* A cash gift of $ 30,000

In addition to the above, each town with a population of over 200,000 could have been allocated a cash donation of $35 million for libraries, $35 million for schools, and another $40 million for hospitals!

All these astronomical sums were spent instead on a war which lasted over five years and touched four continents!

If ever there is another war on this scale, what would become of humanity?

When the cross-bow was designed, people feared that it would lead to mass-killing. Then came gunpowder—and canons, capable of causing instant death of hundreds of people. Then we invented nuclear weapons—whose destructive power we are yet to fathom. Now we only talk on WMD—weapons of mass destruction. There is talk too, of biological warfare, raining cruel diseases and infections upon a whole nation and its people.

The hearts of people and nations are filled with hatred and selfishness. Wars continue to mutilate humanity.

When will lasting and abiding peace become a reality on earth?

Life is a Challenge...
Life is So Unpredictable...

It is said that eclipses and thunderstorms drove fear and horror into the hearts of our ancestors, who feared that such natural phenomena were actually the manifestation of God's wrath against the sins of mankind. Every eclipse and every shooting star, according to them, foretold the fall of emperors and the decline of nations.

For us in the third millennium A.D. natural disasters and calamities have become annual occurrences like summer vacations and the New Year. Hurricanes, typhoons, El Nino and Tsunami—these 'new' disasters have been added to earthquakes, volcanic eruptions and landslides.

Even apart from such obvious natural calamities, experts tell us that planet earth is facing an unprecedented threat due to environmental degradation. Whole species are threatened with extinction; streams, rivers and even seas are becoming polluted; ground water is contaminated; and the very air we breathe is choking our lungs. The ozone layer is being depleted, and the life-giving warmth of the sun, we are told, will soon cause skin cancer due to harmful ultraviolet rays. Summers are hotter, winters are colder, and it no longer rains—it pours, it floods cities!

What will happen to the earth?

How will we survive?

Where are we heading?

Orphaned Humanity

Humanity is like an orphan crying in the night, crying for the light. This is why eminent thinkers, philosophers and scientists tell us that civilization has become sick. Today, wherever you turn, there is passion for power; lust for fame; greed for gold. Today the nations seem to be wandering in a jungle of darkness, where might is right. Today, humanity stands amidst the ruins of values and ideals. Mother Nature shudders with horror, while her children are busy building weapons of death and destruction.

What is the cause?

Very many years ago, a young man came to meet my Master, Sadhu Vaswani. He was utterly desolate and downcast, and he said to the Master, "I am just thirty years old, and I am an utter failure! I have lost my job.

My ancestral property is mortgaged. My wife has left me, and I am unable to support my old mother. I am utterly frustrated with life. What shall I do?"

Sadhu Vaswani said to him, "You are not the pathetic weakling that you take yourself to be! You are not poor and broken! You are like the prodigal son who has drifted away from his rich father and does not know how infinitely rich he is."

The young man was bemused. "Excuse me," he stammered. "Who is this rich father you are speaking of? My own father passed away five years ago—and he only left behind debts which I am yet to pay off!"

Sadhu Vaswani smiled and said to him, "I am speaking of our Heavenly Father. He is the Father of us all. And He is the source of all supply. He is the source of all that you and I will ever need or desire. He is the source of prosperity, plenty and peace. He is the source of happiness and harmony. He is the source of love and joy, strength and wisdom, power and security. All you need to do is turn to Him—and you will lack nothing!"

Alas—that is exactly what we cannot or will not do!

The Swiss psychiatrist Carl Jung states, "Civilization today has become sick because man has alienated himself from God."

Is not this the worst malady that afflicts modern man? We live in an age of unprecedented scientific progress and technological development. Science has given us so many blessings, so many comforts, so many conveniences, so many gadgets. But alas, all this has only inflated our ego and blinded us to the truth about ourselves—that we are all God's children.

I think the greatest affliction of modern civilization is that we are moving away from God, and the awareness that we are His children.

Some young atheists even say, "We have no need of God. There is nothing man cannot do on his own. Man has been able to set his foot on the moon. Man's rockets go flying past the distant planets. Man has been able to station satellites in space. Who needs God today?"

God is the source and sustainer of life. And man cannot live a healthy life physically, mentally, morally, spiritually, so long as he cuts himself off from God. It is very easy to drive the spirit out of the door—but once you have done that, life loses its flavor; the 'salt of life' grows flat.

Yes. This is exactly what has happened to us today. Life has lost its flavor; the salt of life has grown flat; today more and more people are beginning to declare that life has no meaning—therefore, what is the point in living?

Thanks to material progress, we have more and more 'means' today—but lesser and lesser *meaning*. Material opulence is increasing—but the number of suicides goes up too!

Internet, broadband … high-speed communication … but increasing hypertension!

Gyms and elevators … but more heart diseases!

Megabytes, gigabytes … millions of data cells being transferred in nanoseconds … but more misunderstandings and absence of real communication!

Mobiles, SMS, flat screens, LCD, plasma TVs, laptops, palmtops, greater digital resolution … but no time for family or friends!

Five star hospitals, state of the art equipment, more comfortable wards … but less care and compassion!

Higher standard of living … but reduced quality of life!

What is the cure?

When Things Fall Apart ...

Every era, every age, every century in the past has had to face its own fears, insecurities and uncertainties. You only have to turn the pages of history to realize that our ancestors have gone through it all:

* The ancient civilizations of the West were destroyed by 'barbarians' who attacked their countries and ruthlessly destroyed their cities.

* Some great empires like the Babylonian, 'self—destructed' as it were, under the weight of their own hedonism and extreme vices.

* The Old Testament tells us of doomed cities—one could say damned cities in the literal sense—like Sodom and Gomorrah which God is said to have destroyed with brimstone and fire: for they had given in to utter sin and vice.

* The early Christians had to face persecution and torture from the Roman Empire. An entire community faced martyrdom because of their faith.

* Prophet Mohammad and his followers faced similar persecution from other tribes in Arabia.

* The Crusades—probably the first and the longest running, bitterly fought religious war– pitted Christians against Islamic nations for the control of what both religions claimed as their own "holy land."

* The notorious 'inquisitions' carried out by the Roman Catholic Church in the 12th and 13th centuries, actually targeted dissidents within the church. Outstanding men and women of true faith—like St. Joan—actually perished in this 'legal' onslaught—only to be resurrected by a reformed church much later.

* The original 'invaders' of India like Mohammed Gazni looted, ravaged and plundered the north of the country. A reign of terror was unleashed on a peaceful land.

* Battles and wars for political supremacy were constant in Europe – between France and England, between Prussia and the Austro-Hungarian empire, between Russia and Germany and so on—ultimately culminating in World War I—which was thought of as the 'war to end all wars'!

* When Galileo and Charles Darwin put forward their revolutionary concepts, they were met with disbelief and anger—and condemned as irreligious.

* From the seventeenth century, the horrifying practice of slave-trade began to flourish. Africans were bought and sold by powerful white Europeans who 'transported' them en masse to work on plantations in the 'New World'—America. Man's inhumanity to man assumed a new dimension of horror with this practice, which would later plunge America into a civil war.

* Infectious diseases in those days, were practically incurable. Plague, cholera and other ailments laid waste entire cities in the days when medical aid was unavailable to the poor.

* When diseases were under control, natural disasters like floods and draughts and famine wiped out thousands of lives. The distinguished economist Malthus actually propounded the theory that when human population grew rapidly, such mass loss of lives would actually become inevitable.

* The Industrial revolution brought its store of misery to a largely agrarian world society. The world woke up to new evils like exploitation, urbanization and the beginning of environmental degradation.

I could go on and on, listing the crises and challenges that humanity has faced down the ages. But I would like to give you a powerful image portrayed by the poet W.B. Yeats, writing in 1919. These lines are from his prophetic, visionary poem, "The Second Coming":

> Turning and turning in the widening gyre
> The falcon cannot hear the falconer
> Things fall apart, the centre cannot hold

One cannot help being struck by the horror of anarchy and disorder conveyed in these lines. The image of the falcon which cannot hear the falconer is suggestive of so many things—loss of control, loss of discipline, disintegration of order and rule of law; some would even say, of mankind drifting away from God; of a civilization that is spinning crazily towards its own disintegration.

"Things fall apart" became such a powerful expression that the distinguished Nigerian writer Chinua Achebe, chose it to be the title of his award-winning novel—which portrays the colonial exploitation of Africa and the total destruction of the rich native culture and religion of Nigerian society.

How sad and terrible human history has been when we view it from this perspective!

But the purpose of my account is not to plunge you into pessimism! I only wish to draw your attention to the fact that problems and crises and disasters are not the prerogatives of the modern age alone. Every age, every generation has been overwhelmed by the rapidity and the negative impact of the changes they see around them—and every age has felt that doomsday is drawing closer; that human civilization cannot take more!

But the remarkable, undeniable fact is that we have survived; the planet is still in one piece; history marches on; human civilization is still making rapid strides!

How was this possible?

We learnt to face the challenges of life—that's how!

It has not been an easy ride. Humanity stumbled and fell, not once, but several times, along the way. When we failed to learn the bitter lessons life was teaching us, history had to repeat itself—and we learnt things the hard way. We struggled, we quarreled, we ruined our prospects; in the process valuable lives were lost, precious institutions were destroyed, and values and ideals were sacrificed at the altar of material necessity. Humanity was wounded; civilization was bleeding; we wandered in the darkness of ignorance and strife; and we learnt our lessons.

The corridors of history, the pathways of life are strewn with challenges. There is scarcely a day when we do not have to meet some challenge or the other!

A Vision for the Future

Thus far, I have been telling you about the problems and challenges that confront humanity today. It is undeniable that we are passing through a period of crisis. Unrest is deepening in the nations of the world. There is a wild race for weapons and missiles, battleships and bomber jets and sophisticated arms and ammunition.

Today, there is a craze for 'big' and 'great'. Little things, alas, do not satisfy us anymore. It would seem that our very egos have become inflated! We want to amass larger fortunes, build bigger structures, found bigger institutions, and write bigger volumes! I am afraid all this leads to 'bigger' and greater unhappiness!

Even more worrying is the moral decay that has set in. The moral base of public life has been shattered; values are no longer respected.

All over the world, today, there is a cry for a new world order; a new life. For men and women, young and old are tired of the present order. The cry comes from temples and churches, from factories and farms, from homes and offices, from souls seeking peace, and hearts full of aspiration for a better future.

But let me tell you—there is hope for us all! I believe a new age is dawning, a new age when love and peace will be established upon this earth. I don't merely believe it, I can almost hear the new age knocking on the doors of our hearts. All we need are the blessed ones who will open the door to the new age!

Very often, I am asked the question: What is your vision of the 21st century?

My answer—and my vision—are very simple! Mine is a vision of a world without war, a world without *want*. A world in which every human being can live a life of dignity, with all the necessities of life provided, and can hold his head high. A world in which peace prevails among nations and harmony among the peoples of the earth. A world in which the right to live is guaranteed to every creature that breathes the breath of life.

Mine is the vision of a world in which the truth is recognized that life and all its bounties, all that we are and all that we have—our time and talents, knowledge and wisdom, experience and influence, prestige and power, wealth and strength, indeed, life itself —is a *loan* given to us, to be passed on to those whose need is greater than ours!

I am convinced that we are standing on the threshold of a new age of love and peace that will see all nations and all people united by the bonds of brotherhood.

Today, we have arrived at a stage where, nations and individuals alike must learn to understand one another— to make peace or perish! There is no other choice!

II
THE THREE DIMENSIONS OF PEACE

Peace Be With You!

Peace! It is as if we have become immune to this word! Although it is frequently in use, it seems so alien to us in reality. But is not peace the ultimate quest of every human heart? Are you not all lovers of peace? Peace is what we all crave. Peace is what humanity has piteously cried for, age after age. Peace, peace, peace—in this one word you have the secret, the answer to all your questions.

The rabbis of the Talmud used lavish words of praise to indicate the significance of peace:

Great is peace, for God's name is peace ... Great is peace, for it encompasses all blessings ... Great is peace, for even in times of war, peace must be sought ... Great is peace seeing that when the Messiah is to come, He will commence with peace, as it is said, "How beautiful upon the mountains are the feet of the messenger of good tidings, who announces peace."

—Isa. 52:7

I think of blessed Jesus. Of him we are told that as he traveled from place to place, from town to town, from hamlet to hamlet, there was one word he uttered again and again, in Aramaic, which was his mother tongue. Wherever he entered a house or left it, whenever he addressed a crowd of men, whenever someone came to him for blessing or healing, he uttered this one word: '*Shalomica, Shalomica!*' Peace! Peace!

I think of the great prophet of Arabia, the prophet of Islam, Prophet Muhammad. We read of him, that one day a man came to him and said, "O Prophet of Allah! Give me a command!" And the Prophet said to him, "Be at peace with all." The question was repeated several times, but the answer was the same: "Be at peace with all."

Even the very word *Islam* is derived from a root, which means peace. Etymology tells us that *Islam* is derived from *sin-lam-mim*, which carries the basic meaning of safety and peace.

I think of the great rishis of India, the great rishis of Aryavanta, who held peace very dear in their hearts. That is why; at the end of every Vedic prayer we have the sacred chant—*Om Shanti Shanti Shanti!*

Scholars tell us that the sacred word is uttered thrice to heal us, protect us, give us freedom from three kinds of ills that destroy our peace:

Adhyatmika – the mental, physical, and spiritual troubles and ills that we cause ourselves.

Adhibhautikam – the troubles and ills caused to us by others, outside of us.

Aadhidhaivikam – the troubles caused to us by natural phenomena such as rain, storm, thunder, lightning, fire, floods, etc.

The three-fold recital *Om Shanti Shanti Shanti* brings us peace by relieving us from all three evils.

Om Shanti Shanti Shanti, the sweet serene feeling of goodwill to all, the sweet serene feeling of positivity to all, the sweet serene feeling of peace to all. *Shanti* is *Shalomica*! *Shalomica* is peace! *Om Shanti* peace, *peace be unto you!* This is the benediction that the nations need today. Of such peace, did Jesus speak when he said: *Blessed are the peacemakers!*

THE FIRST DIMENSION: PEACE WITHIN

How May We Attain Peace?

Throughout the centuries, nations have sought many ways to attain peace. Many methods have they tried—force, aggression—yes! They have claimed that they have fought wars to bring about peace! They have also tried negotiations, conferences, treaties and 'peace' talks. They have had a League of Nations in the past, they have United Nations now. But where O where is Peace … true peace?

I believe peace must have three dimensions: Peace within our own selves; peace among the nations; and peace with nature!

The first dimension of peace: Peace within.

What is peace? I may tell you what peace is in many words, but all descriptions will fail and you will not understand those words until you have felt peace in the heart within!

Like love, peace must be felt!

One of the questions people ask me most often is: Do you think it is possible for *anyone* to lead a life of peace in these troubled times?

My reply is: It is not only possible; it is your *birthright.* Yes, *ananda*, bliss, the peace that passeth, nay, surpasseth understanding is your birthright! You are a child of God—and he is the source of eternal bliss, unending bliss. The moment you realize that you are a child of God, you will let nothing affect you. All you need to do is forget yourself—and realize your true self as a child of God. When we forget this outer self, transcend the phenomenal, material world, we draw closer to the real, inner self, which is peace.

In Chapter Two of the *Bhagavad Gita,* the Lord gives us the wonderful picture of the *stitha prajna,* the balanced man:

> A man with a disciplined mind, who moves among sense objects, with the senses under control and free from attachment and aversion, he rises to a state of *prasadam,* peace. … Having attained peace, there is for him an end of all sorrow; of such a man of peace the understanding soon attaineth equilibrium.
>
> —Bhagavad Gita, Chapter II, 64, 65

These *slokas* emphasize the great truth that only a person who is *not* disturbed by the incessant flow of desires can achieve peace; not the man who strives to satisfy desires. These *slokas*, I am told, were very dear to the heart of Mahatma Gandhi. He had them recited everyday at his prayer meetings.

Yes, there is truly one way of achieving peace of mind. That is to attain the realization that all that happens, happens according to the will of God.

Why is it that we lose our peace of mind? Because our wishes, our desires, are crossed. We want a particular thing to be done in a particular manner. When it happens in a different way, perhaps in exactly the opposite way, our peace is lost.

This is exactly what happens in Shakespeare's *King Lear*. The old king has already decided to share his kingdom equally among his three daughters; but, at the moment of actually giving it all away, he is possessed with the fond desire—to hear his daughters proclaim how much they love him!

The two elder daughters, who are anxious to secure their share, rise to the occasion. They utter flowery speeches to show how much they love him; much of their sentiments are exaggerated and false.

The youngest daughter, Cordelia, is disgusted by this public display. Loving and loyal, she is nevertheless stubborn and independent. She decides that she will not "heave her heart into her mouth" to proclaim how much she loves her father.

"I love you as much as a daughter should love her father" is all she says. The old king is disappointed; his ego crumbles; this is not the way he wanted things to happen; he expected something quite different; that his favorite daughter, Cordelia, would emerge the winner in this public 'elocution' contest.

When Cordelia refuses to oblige him, he not only loses his temper and his peace of mind, he also loses all sense of balance and proportion. In fact, Shakespeare goes on to show that he eventually loses his reason and his sanity!

Why do we feel upset, frustrated, disappointed? Because we are attached, because we are involved. If I do my work, if I live my life as if I am playing a part, I would not be upset.

If something happens in a play, do you feel upset? Supposing another 'character' in the play scolds you or speaks ill of you, do you get angry? No! You know you have to play your part well.

If only we can realize this, that we are all actors in the drama of life; that the role you are playing has been given to you by the Cosmic Director – we will never, ever feel upset. We will not be entangled.

But, of course, there's a catch. In the cosmic drama of life, you have to play a double role. You have to be an actor and you also have to be a spectator. You have to watch the play unfolding before your eyes—and you also have to act. If you are able to do this, you will not lose your peace of mind.

It is not easy to do this —maintain your inner equilibrium at all times and in all situations.

Sadhu Vaswani used to tell us, "God upsets our plans to set up his own. And his plans are always perfect."

If I have the faith that whatever has happened to me is according to the plan of the Highest, that there is some hidden good in it for me, I will not be upset! Sadhu Vaswani also used to say, "Every disappointment is His appointment. And He knows best."

Once you realize this, there is no more frustration, no more unhappiness. You abide in a state of tranquility and peace. You may not be able to achieve this straight away. It is a process through which you must move.

One easy way of attaining peace of mind, is to sit in silence everyday for ten to fifteen minutes, and explain this one thing to yourself: "Whatever happens, happens according to the will of God. If something happens contrary to my desires, it has happened according to God's will. Therefore, there must be some good in it for me."

Explain this to your mind everyday. "O mind; why is it that you lose your peace?

May I say to you, you will get peace of mind if you give your own 'piece' to others! The great poet saint, Saint Tulsidas, says:

Tulsi is sansar mein kar leejiye do kaam
Dene ko tukda bhala, lene ko Hari naam.

"Keep on giving," the saint tells us. "When you have learnt to give, you have learnt to live aright. Then peace automatically wakes up in the heart within."

It is only because we are so self-centered that our peace is disturbed. Peace is our original nature. We are made of peace. Each one of us is *Sat Chit Ananda*. *Ananda* is the joy, the bliss that no ending knows. This is our original state—we have only to get back to it!

I am sure you must have seen on several occasions that when your mind is disturbed, and you do a little painting, or play a little tune, or sing a song, you find that peace fills you all at once. Why? Because you forget yourself in this creative work. Likewise, when we move out of ourselves and give joy to those who are in need of joy, we forget ourselves and give joy to those who are in need of joy, we forget ourselves—we forget to be self-centered— and peace is ours! When we forget the outer self, we draw closer to the real, the inner self, which is peace.

We live in an excited, agitated world—a world beset with stress and strain. This intensified stress and strain manifests itself physically as heart disease, hypertension and nervous breakdown. Doctors agree that the cause of such ailments is psychological rather than physical.

The great athletic trainer William Muldoon once said, "People do not die of disease, they die of internal combustion."

Our ancestors in India were fond of saying: "*Man durust, tan durust.*" *If the mind is at peace, the body is bound to be hale and hearty.*

It all sounds so simple and logical; with peace our minds are balanced, our bodies healthy and our hearts are happy. Life doesn't seem like a challenge anymore!

So let us move ahead to the discovery of true peace.

May I offer you now, eight steps to interior peace?

Eight Steps to Interior Peace
Step 1: Begin the Day with God

"Can you have your concert first and tune your instrument afterwards?" a spiritual teacher asks us. The answer is obviously no— we cannot. "Therefore," he continues, "Begin your day with God."

A long time ago, I came across a billboard which advertised a nerve-tonic. "How you feel tomorrow depends on what you take today," it proclaimed.

How true are these words when applied to our daily life! Our tomorrows depend a great deal on our todays. And our todays depend on what we do with our mornings.

The first thing we do on getting up in the morning shapes the entire day. Does it not stand to reason that we should begin the day right?

Many people I'm afraid, spoil their mornings by waking up with a feeling of restlessness, irritability and tension. How sad this is.

A sister once said to me "When I come awake early in the morning, the first thing that comes into my mind is all the accumulated work I have to face. The first thought that I think on most days is, 'I don't want to get up' or 'I don't think that I can cope. 'Sometimes I even wish I were ill, so that I can take medical leave with a clear conscience, and just stay in bed."

How sad it is, that we should begin the day wishing that it had *not* begun at all!

Many young people say that they "hate getting out of bed in the mornings." To them I would like to say that every new day is a special gift from God to you. 24 hours times 60 minutes times 60 seconds offered to you to do what you like. A brand new day which you can use as you will. You can throw it all away—or use it for your own good and the good of other people around you. What you do with it is important—for, after all, it is a whole day of *your* life. Don't you think you ought to begin it on a better note than simply thinking, "I hate getting out of bed"?

Every morning, when you awake, there is a choice before you: you can choose optimism, faith, positive thinking and right attitude; or you can choose pessimism, defeat, negative thinking and despair. What would you choose? Here is a beautiful way in which an American writer, Dan Custer, puts it:

> Every morning is a fresh beginning. Everyday is the world made new. Today is a new day. Today is my world made new. ... I shall make of this day, each moment of this day, a heaven on earth. This is my day of opportunity.

Begin the day well—and God will take care of the rest of the day!

I know of a family of seven members. At an early hour of the morning, all the seven meet together and begin the day by picking up a line from a scripture or the writings of a great one. They ponder over it in silence for a few minutes: then each member of the family shares his/her reflections on the thought.

The mother then lays the table for the morning meal, saying: "You have had your breakfast with God. Now you can have your bread."

"Breakfast with God" should be the most important item in our daily routine—a daily appointment you must never ever miss!

I read of a busy, wealthy man. He was always on the move, attending numerous meetings, flying from place to place, meeting so many people. However, despite his hectic schedule, he always managed to set aside some time, he said, to speak to God first thing in the morning and the last thing—as he slipped into sleep.

Early one morning, he was told that he had a very important visitor waiting to meet him.

"He must wait a little longer," the man said. "I have an appointment with God right now."

Have you visited the offices of powerful, influential people, VVIPs whom hundreds of us long to meet if only for a few minutes? They often have super-efficient secretaries and ever—vigilant guards to keep people away. But when someone close to the VIP arrives, the staff knows that he or she must not be stopped, and the visitor is allowed to walk right in, even while a room full of people waits anxiously.

Why not take a leaf from these rich and powerful people whom we all love to emulate? Set aside all else— cancel all other 'visits' and 'appointments' to give first preference to God, early in the morning. Begin your day with God—and He will take care of the rest!

Everyday, as you wake up in the morning, let there be a prayer on your lips, a simple prayer. Let me share with you the prayer that I offer to God:

O Lord! This new day comes to me as a gift from Thy spotless hands. You have taken care of me throughout the night, and I am sure You will keep watch over me throughout the day. Praise be to Thee, O Lord. Blessed be Thy Name. Blessed be Thy Name. Blessed be Thy Name!

You can reword this prayer if you like, in your own way. But make sure you begin the day by remembering God – with a prayer on your lips.

Many of my friends tell me, "The moment we get out of bed, we rush off to brush our teeth and wash our face and go through the rest of the morning routine!

And then, may be five minutes, ten minutes later, we remember that we have *not* said our prayer as you taught us to do!"

If you are one of these people, let me say to you— don't let this stop you. Even if you have forgotten to remember God first thing, even if you have forgotten to say your early morning prayer—go *back* to bed and do it! If you do this once or twice, it will become a habit. Go back to bed, get under your sheets, close your eyes, and thank God for the gift of a brand new day. And then, carry on with your routine activities.

I know a lady who keeps dozens of 'Thank you' cards in her desk. Whenever someone does her a good turn— it may be a favor at work, it may be a kind inquiry about her loved ones, a birthday or a New year greeting—she promptly dashes off one of her Thank you cards to them.

What about you? Whenever a friend brings you a small gift, you are pleased and touched, aren't you? You say, "How kind of you," or "Thank you!" and you express your appreciation.

But we do not thank the Lord for His many gifts to us. We take Him for granted—we take His blessings for granted.

If you wish to have peace of mind, you must not take anything for granted. Therefore, remember to thank the Lord for everything—and thank Him everyday, first thing in the morning. And the very first thing you should thank Him for is the gift of a new day.

We hear of so many people who went to sleep as usual—but failed to wake up the next morning. Death claimed them during their sleep.

Every night, as we sleep, we are not even conscious of our breathing, but God watches over us, watches over each breath that we inhale and exhale.

I know there are many things to irritate the average man or woman, even as the new day begins. You have to rush off to catch a bus or train; may be you have to drive to work, maneuvering through heavy traffic; but even before you are ready, there are other irritations; somebody is using the bathroom—and you have to wait. This is enough to upset many people!

A priest was visiting the home of a young couple, newcomers to his parish. He was eager to get the family into the habit of regular Church-going. He was invited to the dinning room, where the couple's only child, a boy of six years, was been given regular breakfast—the mother was anxious to make him drink at least a glass of milk before the school bus arrived.

The priest decided that he would start on the boy right away. "Tell me, little one," he said, "Do you know where God lives?"

To his surprise, the boy nodded vigorously and said, "Yes, I do".

Taken back, the priest thought that the boy had already been told about the importance of the Church. So he said, "Where?"

"God lives in our bathroom," the boy asserted solemnly, unaware of the bombshell he was dropping.

"How…what… What do you mean?" stammered the priest, shell-shocked. "Who told you this?"

"Well, every morning Papa stands before the bathroom door and yells, 'God, are you still in there?' so I guess God must be in there!"

Put aside all your irritations for a moment when you get up. Let your mind focus on God. Let your mind be calm, unruffled and serene. Tell yourself, this is the first waking moment of a brand new day—and your most priceless possession, peace of mind, must not be taken away from you now.

Even as you try to focus on your mind on God, you will find a hundred thoughts crowding in. Most of them are not really useful or constructive. Therefore, after you have expressed your gratitude to God, let your mind dwell for a minute or two on a great thought—a great saying—a line or a *sloka* from a scripture.

Take up a *sloka* from the Gita, a verse from the Bible, or a *sura* from the holy Quran. Or choose any other text or scripture that is dear to you—and dwell on it.

If you do this at the dawn of a new day you will find that your mind is repeatedly drawn to this text during the course of the day. This will make a great difference to the state of your mind.

Begin the day with God. Take up a great thought of a great one and reflect upon it. Repeat this great thought whenever you can, throughout the day.

If you truly wish to live each day fully—successfully—let me also urge you to practice silence, at least for a brief while, every morning.

Every morning, preferably at the same time and at the same place, sit in silence for a few minutes. Devote at least fifteen minutes to this at first, if you can spare the time, the period may gradually be increased to at least an hour.

I can anticipate some of your reactions to this suggestion: "One *hour!*" One *whole* hour. Dada must be joking!"

I am not joking! Benjamin Franklin once told us, "Time is money." The English writer Arnold Bennett went one step further:

> Time is the inexplicable raw material of everything. Without it nothing is possible. The supply of time is truly a daily miracle. You wake up in the morning, and lo! Your purse is magically filled with 24 hours... No one can take it from you. It is un-stealable. And no one receives either more or less than you receive. Wealth or genius is never rewarded by even an extra hour a day.

Arnold Bennett goes on to argue that out of 24 hours in any given day, most of us work from nine to five—i.e. eight hours a day. Some of us might claim that we work *ten* hours. Fine. What happens to the remaining fourteen hours? If we sleep for seven hours, what happens to the remaining seven? Are we aware of how these valuable hours are spent?

We make such a fuss about the 8-10 hours we put in at work. But many of us, alas, do not give all we can to our work. We begin with reluctance, and we end with relief. And rarely do we work full steam.

What is even worse, we regard nine-to-five as 'work'— and the hours before and after work are dismissed as a margin, or a sort of foreword and afterward, with not much consequence. Thus, nearly 16 hours of the day are uncounted for!

If you work from nine to five, you have sixteen hours with which you can cultivate your body, mind, soul and your fellow human beings. During these sixteen hours you are free! You are not a wage-earner! Your time is your own!

Do you still think you have 'no time' to devote or fifteen minutes of silence every morning? I am sure you will find time, if you so wish—and I can assure you it will be time well spent.

Begin the day with gratitude to God; reflect for a few minutes on the great thought of a great one! And spend some time in silence every morning. You will find that you have made a sound investment for your own interior peace!

I have always maintained that prayer is not a complicated affair. It is a very simple matter, as simple as talking to a friend. All we have to do is close our eyes, shut out the world, open our heart and call out to Him and here He is in front of us.

Meditation and reflection need not be difficult either. I would define meditation very simply thus: It is directing our attention to eternal things and keeping it there for a while.

Within each one of us is the realm we seek—the realm of peace! Through practice we can, at will, enter into this realm and claim the peace that is our birthright. We can contact God, who is the source of all Peace and Joy. When we do so, we become conscious of the infinite power and a wondrous peace, and realize that everything is perfect and in its own place!

To begin with, when we sit in silence, let us think of a world very much like the world we live in—but which is free of all disorder and chaos. A world in which everything is done with love, for love's sake, for helping other people; a world in which everything comes to pass in the right way, at the right time, in a perfectly harmonious manner. As we visualize such a world, we will find the perfection and peace of God flowing into our lives like a perennial river.

When I ask you to begin the day with God, the idea is to contact God who is the source of happiness, health and success. Go to the source for everything you need. Tap on this source for success, joy and peace. Make God a partner in your daily activities—and you will find miracles happen in your daily life. You will grow in the assurance that there is no problem that you and God cannot solve together; there is no situation which you and God cannot handle together!

We are told that St. Theresa wanted to build an orphanage. At that time, she had only three shillings in her pocket. She said to those who ridiculed her: "With three shillings Theresa can do nothing; but with God and three shillings there is nothing that Theresa cannot do!"

When Sadhu Vaswani was inspired with the vision to found a new type of school – indeed, a new movement in education—he had only a two-*paise* coin in his pocket.

In the early hours of the dawn of June 4, 1933, he kindled the sacred *havan* fire, and announced the opening of St. Mira's School for Girls in Hyderabad, Sind, in what was then undivided India.

Handing over the two-*paise* coin to the secretary of the *Sakhi Satsang*, the voluntary service organization which he had founded, Sadhu Vaswani said to the assembled devotees, "Our school will be started with this blessed coin."

Sadhu Vaswani began his school with an early morning prayer and a two-*paise* coin: the Bank of Providence took care of the rest. Devotees, volunteers and philanthropists came forward to help him. A core fund was quickly established. Able, willing, well-qualified devotees offered their services free, to teach and work in the school—in the same spirit of service and sacrifice urged by the saintly founder. This is how the first Mira school came into being.

On June 4, 1933 in the sacred hour of the dawn was planted the seed that has today grown into a vast sheltering tree. Today, the Mira Movement in Education has over ten institutions located all over India. Thousands of students are educated in the Mira Institutions—from the pre-primary to the postgraduate level. The institutions revere their sacred Founder, and know that his spirit still presides over their daily sanctuary—a unique Mira feature, which helps us begin our day with God!

The sanctuary is a daily period of devotion, reflection and prayer, with which classes begin in the Mira Institutions. In the sanctuary, the students are educated on the art of living aright. They are taught about the life of the Spirit, inculcated with the wisdom of India's sages and saints, with readings from various sacred texts, and discourses on the art of living aright. The sanctuary is the very foundation of the character-building education that the Mira Institutions strive to impart.

When we begin the day with God, we harness ourselves to the Source of the highest power and energy in the Universe. We give ourselves the best start that we are capable of. We reiterate our utter dependence on God and ensure that He is with us in all that He is with us in all that we do.

I have always believed that the life of silence and prayer must be blended with the life of work. On no account must we fail to fulfill our worldly duties and obligations. What we achieve by beginning the day with God is this: momentarily, we withdraw ourselves from our worldly concerns and give ourselves wholly to God. Then we must return to our work—and pour into it the vitality of the Spirit!

When you begin the day with God, you will find yourself remembering Him throughout the day. In the midst of your work, you can pause, and out of the depths of a love-filled heart, say to God: "I need You God! I cannot do without You!"

So I urge you once again. Begin the day with God. And hold fast to Him throughout the day. He will fill your day with the peace that passeth, surpasseth understanding.

Step 2: Let Your Mind Rest in God

The second step to interior peace centers around the words of the great Jewish prophet Isaiah:

Thou wilt keep him at peace whose mind is stayed on Thee.

The Prophet was speaking out of experience. He had discovered the secret of true and lasting peace. He must have found that every time his mind stayed on the Lord, every time he felt he was in the presence of the Lord, he was at peace.

Thou wilt keep Him in perfect peace whose mind is stayed on Thee!

There was a very wealthy man who came to meet Sadhu Vaswani. He said to the Master, "I have all that

I need and more. I am grateful to God who has blessed me with all the wealth of the world. But…"

The Master waited for him to continue.

"I have big mansions to live in—wherever in the world my business interests are located. And my businesses are all doing very well. My children lack nothing—they attend the best schools and universities in the world…

"I have everything the world can give—but I am not happy. Can you please tell me what is the reason?"

Sadhu Vaswani's reply was a simple one. He said to him, "You are not happy because you lack peace of mind."

Ashantasya Kutah Sukham! For the unpeaceful, how can there be happiness, says Sri Krishna in the *Bhagavad Gita*. How can anyone be happy if he is not at peace?

The man was not ready to give up so easily. He persisted, "Why do I not have peace of mind?"

"Because your mind is restless," Sadhu Vaswani replied.

Our minds are restless. They are restless like storm-tossed boats. Our minds wander here and there. Our feet may be firmly planted on the earth—in Pune, New York, London or Singapore. But our minds wander to the four corners of the globe!

How many months, how many years it takes for a rocket to reach a distant planet like Saturn? But if you think of that planet, it is there in your mind—you are there in thought. Your thought moves faster than sound or light. Your mind will not be confined by any limits or barriers. The mind is its own space; the mind is its own power. This is certainly a good thing for the mind.

But the negative aspect of this is that the mind is restless. It cannot be still; its feet are burning; it cannot stop; it will not stay in one place; it keeps on wandering!

Thou wilt keep him in perfect peace whose mind is stayed on Thee!

Can you try a little exercise? Every time you become aware that the mind wanders, quietly, gently, lovingly, sweetly, bring the mind back to the Divine Presence. It is not easy! Even as you become aware that the mind is wandering, we are wandering with the mind! However, do your best to stop the wandering mind in its tracks, and bring it lovingly back to the Divine Presence.

Do not attempt to fight the mind—for the mind can be a formidable enemy! Make friends with it. Say to it gently, as you would tell a stubborn child, that it would be good for it to focus on the Divine Presence. Allow your mind to savor the peace that this can bring. Say to it, "See, see how happy we are sitting in His Divine Presence! He will keep us in perfect peace when we rest in Him. Why can't we sit at His Lotus feet, and experience the bliss of life?"

Repeat this simple exercise over a period of three to six months. You will be amazed at the change that this brings about in your life! Your life will become new!

When your mind wanders, and you become aware of it, bring it back to the Divine Presence.

Thou wilt keep him in perfect peace whose mind is stayed on Thee!

It was Meher Baba, the Sufi mystic who said: "A mind that is fast is sick. A mind that is slow is sound. A mind that is still is Divine." If you wish to realize your own Divinity, slow the mind down, still the mind and rest the mind in the Divine Presence.

Let me make one thing clear. I am not encouraging you to cultivate emptiness of mind. I am asking you to fill your mind with the Divine Presence. A vacant mind, as Dr. Johnson warns us, invites dangerous inmates, as a deserted mansion tempts vagrants and outcasts to take up their abode in its desolate rooms. Let me repeat: Do not just empty your mind – fill it with all that is noble and good.

The *Annapurna Upanishad* tells us of a great sage who seeks Truth by withdrawing his mind from sense perceptions. To his surprise, even while he reflects on the steadiness of his mind, he realizes that although it is withdrawn, it is still extremely restless. This is what he says about the mind:

> It wanders from a cloth to a pot and thence to a big cart. The mind wanders among objects as a monkey does from tree to tree.

> — (Annapurana Upanishad III—6)

The mind is a monkey! The ancient rishi found it wandering from a cloth to a pot to a cart. As for us in the 21st century, we are so 'advanced' that we have a million 'sophisticated' things for the wandering mind to latch on to!

Recently, a survey conducted among young students in urban India revealed that many of them spent on an average, between 2 to 3 hours *per day* on their cell phones. They said they were not talking all the time; they spent much of their time sending messages.

I once saw someone sending several 'SMSs.' I think we cannot have more apt demonstration of the restless, wandering mind than the act of frantically pressing buttons on a small instrument. Trying to communicate through one's fingertips. I am told that a little boy in the UK damaged his right thumb beyond repair through constant messaging!

It is not just that our mind keeps wandering during the day, it is not at rest even when we fall asleep. I watch people sleeping—and I find their brows knit with frowns. The calm, relaxed look which you find on a baby's face when he is asleep, cannot be found on the face of a sleeping adult. This is because we are worrying, worrying all the time. We cannot switch off our anxiety and worry, even when we are asleep.

Ashantasya Kutah Sukham! The disturbed mind is far from peace. How can it mediate? How can it be at peace? How can it even be happy unless it is established in God?

So it is that Gautama the Buddha tells us in forth right terms:

There is nothing so disobedient as an undisciplined mind; and there is nothing so obedient as a disciplined mind.

Let your mind be the master of your body: therefore, let the mind be disciplined and obedient. As the great Greek dramatist Euripides puts it, "The wavering mind is but a base possession."

All the resources we need are in the mind. And, as Andrew Carnegie tells us, the man who acquires the ability to take full possession of his own mind, may take possession of anything else which he is justly entitled!

Man's mind, it is said, is not just a container to be filled – it is a fire that needs to be kindled. Alas, we take such care about eating well-cooked, hygienically prepared food; we are obsessed about drinking 'purified' water. But look at the trash we feed into our minds!

Thou wilt keep him in perfect peace whose mind is stayed on Thee!

How can we hope to find happiness in the world outside, when we fail to realize that it is centered within our own mind?

Earlier, I spoke of the *yogi* who attempted to withdraw his mind from sense perceptions. I would like to make it clear that I do not expect all of you, my readers, to become hermits and withdraw from the workaday world when I tell you to rest your mind in the Divine Presence. All I am telling you is that focusing on the Divine Presence is an excellent cure for a restless mind.

When your mind is restless, you can achieve nothing; you cannot concentrate on anything worthwhile; you cannot analyze your situation dispassionately; you cannot find a constructive approach to any issues; you cannot solve problems—in short, you cannot face the challenges that life throws before you and hence you cannot face life itself in a proper manner.

Resting your mind in the Divine Presence, as it were, focuses the mind, energizes and vitalizes your intellectual abilities so that you are able to give your best to the situation at hand. This exercise is meant for the working man and woman, business people, executives, teachers and students. It is not withdrawal; it is focusing the mind; it is an attempt to concentrate and thereby acquire greater mind-power; it is an effort to conquer restlessness which scatters our abilities away. Such an effort will not disrupt your work—it will make you work much more efficiently, much more effectively than even before!

Many people tend to set apart work and worship. They feel that there should be a certain time set apart for thinking about God—and a specific time devoted to their work or duty, with which nothing should interfere.

I believe there is a relationship between work and worship. It is this: That work should be done in a spirit of worship; when we worship, we need not neglect our work.

Talking about work and worship, I am reminded of the story of Pundalik. He was such a great devotee of the Lord, that once the Lord Himself came down to earth to have the *darshana*, or holy vision, of this great *bhakta*. Just imagine, the Lord was at the door of Pundalik's humble cottage, waiting for him! At that moment, Pundalik was giving a bath to his parents, who were too old and weak to look after themselves. Seeing the Lord at the door, Pundalik passed a brick to Him and said, "Lord, please stand on this brick and wait, while I attend to my parents."

What did the Lord do? He was not angry. He just stood on the brick and waited patiently, while his humble devotee attended to his duty.

The Lord who stood on the *Vit*, or brick, is known in the state of Maharashtra even today as *Vithoba*.

Many of us find our minds wandering even during prayer—thinking of other things, worldly matters and pending work. If we can think of work even while we pray, why can't we think of God when we are working? This is also a kind of prayer—and it can go on for 24 hours! You can think of God while you are attending to your duty. You can attend to your work, even as you commune with God.

Someone once asked me: Why does the mind wander? My reply was that the cause of wandering is threefold – even as *maya* has three faces, three prongs:

1. The first is pleasure, sense gratification. Pleasure draws us like a magnet. Think of your favorite haunts—the cinema, the theatre, the pub, the club, the bar and so on—all these and many other things fascinate the human mind. They grip your imagination and awaken desires within you. It is desires that make the mind wander.

2. The second face, the second prong of *maya* is wealth. We keep on amassing more and more wealth. We do not even have the time to spend it! Suddenly, death pounces upon us, and leaving our millions behind, we move on, empty-handed, to the Other Shore.

3. The third face of *maya* is name, fame, earthly greatness, power and authority. There are people who shun pleasures and keep away from the pursuit of wealth; but they are very keen on name, fame, prestige and publicity. They too, are prisoners of *maya!*

The perfect man is one whose wandering has ceased!

We may not attain this perfection overnight; but we can and must attempt to focus the wandering mind so that we may harness its power for our own good. I read an anonymous statement which said: Focus on God puts you in touch with the Infinite, so that your mind can grapple with the finite successfully.

Lord Chesterfield once said that a weak, wandering mind becomes like a microscope, which only magnifies trifling things. This is very true. The wandering mind makes mountains out of molehills and perceives insurmountable obstacles on the path of progress. On the other hand, the focused mind acquires the wisdom, strength and power to help us face the challenges of life.

In the words of the Zen Philosopher, Chang Tzu:

If water derives lucidity from stillness, how much more the faculties of the mind! The mind in repose, becomes the mirror of the universe, the speculum of all creation.

Thou wilt keep Him in perfect peace whose mind is stayed on Thee!

Step 3: Be a Lion, Not a Dog

Did you know that there are 'worry experts' who have done much research and analysis on worrying? I heard about 'worry experts' and 'worry professionals' from a friend who told me about an online 'worry club'. They even operate a 24-hour phone line where a worry professional will speak to you and help you to deal with your worry and anxiety. Here is what www.theworryclub.com tells us:

> Talk to a "real, live, professional worrier!" Cheaper than a shrink, more honest than a friend, and much better than hitting your head against a wall. So take the weight of worry and stress off your shoulders and place it on ours. The worry club …where we worry for you so you don't have to!

A 'worry expert' remarks that people are so used to worrying that even when you save them from drowning, put them on the bank safe and dry, and offer them hot chocolate and muffins, they will begin to grow anxious that they may catch a cold!

I have spoken about this online club only to show you how all-pervasive worrying has become today!

People worry about small things and big things. Young people worry about their romantic relationships; young girls even worry about pimples on their face; young men worry about dandruff on their scalp. To us, these might be laughing matters—but not to the worriers. Middle aged people worry about their insurance, investments and repairs to their homes. Old people worry about slipping and falling in the bathroom. There is simply no limit to the worry syndrome.

The trouble with worry is this: once you allow it to enter your system, it often becomes a chronic condition. What I mean is—if you start worrying, you will find it very difficult to stop.

Such is the chronic nature of worriers, that if they momentarily stop worrying, they imagine that there is a disaster about to strike them. In other words, they worry about not being worried! In this state of constant worry you are unable to relax—and in this state of stress and tension, you cannot find solutions to your problems—you cannot face up to the challenges of life!

Henry Neils is a psychological counselor and career assessment expert. He explains how chronic worry can lead to severe stress and eventual burnout by using a simple example. A fork, he points out, is meant for eating; it is likely to last indefinitely. However, if we use a fork to hit nails or dig trenches in the garden, it will break very soon. The key, he observes, is to use things for what they were meant to do.

People are like the fork, Mr. Neils continues. When they do what they are not designed to do, they too, eventually break.

The physical, emotional and psychological effects of worry have been catalogued, analyzed and documented by medical experts and counselors. Worry and anxiety can lead to acidity and ulcers; it may even cause cardiac problems. It may lead us to sickness and exhaustion. We lose the joy of living; we fail to live life fully.

Little wonder that Benjamin Franklin described worry in the following terms:

A god, invisible but omnipotent. It steals the bloom from the cheek and lightness from the pulse; it takes away the appetite and turns the hair grey...

Dr. Tomoaki Sato, M.D, Ph.D. is the Vice-Director of a large medical corporation in Japan. He classifies "problems" or "sources of worry" as follows:

1) There are problems which we need to think about – and actually solve.

For instance, if you are setting out on a long-drawn out expedition, you have to plan all your needs carefully; you need to think about the route; you need to have maps and guides; you must anticipate your material requirements; you must also plan to face unforeseen eventualities. All these require 'thinking about'—if you don't think about them, your expedition will have to break at several points, while you cope with issues which have become problems because you did not plan, prepare to meet them.

Another 'source of worry' which you need to think about is saving for the future, planning your own retirement.

When you approach such issues, you can actually think calmly and rationally and plan constructively to solve them successfully.

In other words, these 'problems' can be solved by thinking and acting calmly.

2) As opposed to this, there are problems which are *not* worth thinking about—because no amount of 'thinking' or 'planning' can solve them.

The classic example of this type of 'problem' is what we call "crying over spilt milk" – regretting, reliving the mistakes and disasters of the past.

If by turning back the pages of the past, we can undo the damage done by our mistakes, we could all devote several hours to this type of worry and regret. But alas, we know only too well that spilt milk cannot be mopped up with a sponge and squeezed into a bowl to make your tea or coffee!

The same applies to the future. Let us say, you are worried that you may contract a fatal illness like cancer at some distant time in your old age. As of now, let us take it you are hale and hearty. You can get a thorough medical check-up done *now* to rule out cancer. You can also adopt a healthy lifestyle and a healthy diet to avoid cancer. But if you persist in imagining that you have cancer after all this, who can help you?

Worrying about the past and the future are futile. As I tell my friends often: The past is a cancelled check; the future is a promissory note. The present is the only cash in hand – we must use it wisely and well!

3) Lastly, there are immediate problems that confront you in the present—they need to be tackled and solved.

For example, there might be a 'growth' in your arm or leg which seems to be abnormal. Of course it must be attended to. You will need to see an expert; you may have to undergo diagnostic tests, including a biopsy. The growth may have to be removed surgically.

This is indeed a serious matter. If you *think* calmly and rationally, and *act* calmly and rationally, you can deal with the issue successfully. But if you begin to *worry* about it, it doesn't help at all!

All we get out of worrying is the 'satisfaction' of being miserable. I am told that there are, unfortunately, some people who enjoy making themselves miserable! This is called "gloomy satisfaction." Unfortunately this 'satisfaction' is taken by your mind and body as mere stress—leading to further complications!

There is no one without 'problems' in life. In fact, a little anxiety is always a good motivation to pass an exam, do well in an interview or even to catch a train. The important thing is that it must not be over done.

People who constantly worry about money, about their job, about their health and their loved ones are reaching negatively to problems. Their anxiety become so pervasive that their lives are taken over by negative feelings, leading to abnormal 'disorders'.

"Don't worry," seems such an inadequate, unsatisfactory, annoying advice to offer such people. Of course they are going to worry. Therefore, experts recommend that they start worrying *smartly, constructively.*

Now let me reassert this: I am not suggesting that you learn to worry constructively or smartly. I am advising you strongly to *empty* your mind of all anxiety and worry. Therefore, learning to worry constructively is, as far as I am concerned, only the first step.

So what do experts have to say to us about it?

1. Learn to 'schedule' your worrying to specific time-bound sessions. Don't worry *all* the time. Set aside a small period of the day for worrying—and postpone all worrying to this session.

2. Even as you are worrying at this duly appointed time, do something healthy—like walking, jogging or a work out.

3. Write your worries down in a diary or a journal. When you face them in black and white, they always seem less formidable.

4. Be prepared for the worst that can happen. This reduces the 'power' that the wrong has over you.

5.   Equally look forward to the best that can happen. After all, a happy ending is always a possibility to the worst situation! This will give you hope and optimism to work towards such an outcome.

6.   Learn to worry over a *specific* issue, rather than indulging in 'global' or 'universal' worrying. For example if you are worrying about your finances, think about how much money you need, how much money you actually have, and how you plan to make more money. Do not worry instead about poverty, debt or bankruptcy!

7.   If there is a specific issue that you can identify— like an illness, a mental disorder or a problematic relationship—try to read up about it. Do a little research on it. For example, it may be your child's dyslexia or attention disorder. Read about it and understand it thoroughly. This will also help you to move towards a constructive solution.

8.   Learn to share your worries with others. They may offer help and advice—or they may just sympathize with you. Either way, you will feel better.

9.   Actively 'deconstruct' your worry. Write your worry on a piece of paper; crumple it; burn it carefully; or throw it into the garbage. This symbolizes your rejection of the worry.

10. Look back at your past worries which you surmounted successfully—or those which turned out to be insignificant! Think of what you were worrying about six weeks ago, six months ago, six years ago, sixteen years ago—you will be amazed to see how they don't matter to you any more! Recall Dr Johnson's words

of wisdom: "Consider, dear sir, how insignificant this will appear ten years hence!"

As I said, this kind of 'constructive' or 'smart' worrying is not an end in itself. It must lead to emptying your mind of all worries, fears and anxieties. How can you achieve this?

Let me begin with an inspirational quote from the Bible:

Do not be anxious about anything, but by prayer and petition, with thanksgiving, present you requests to God. And the peace of God, which transcends all understanding, will guard your heart and mind...

(Philippions 4: 6-7)

In the Gospel according to St. Luke (Ch.10, verses 38-42), Jesus visits the house of the sisters Martha and Mary. Martha gets busy attending to various household chores to make Jesus and his disciples comfortable. As per Mary, she sits at the feet of Jesus, listening eagerly to his words of wisdom. Martha complains about her sister: shouldn't she do something to help? Jesus tells Martha: "You are worried and anxious about many things, but only one thing is needed. Mary has chosen what is better, and it will not be taken away from her."

What was it that freed Mary from the anxiety and fretful activity that kept her sister so 'busy'? Mary chose to focus on Jesus—and on Jesus *alone*; to listen to his every word. In the process, she ignored the demands of hospitality. She was not being irresponsible; she was not trying to shirk her duties; she had her own priorities.

She would listen to Jesus first—everything else could be done later.

This incident teaches us a valuable lesson. Put God first. He will automatically free us from our worries, and take care of all our 'concerns' and 'problems.' There is a beautiful line in the *Sukhmani Sahib*, a Sikh Scripture which I love to meditate on:

Avar tyag tu tisay chitar.

Renounce everything; throw out everything; don't think of anything – but meditate on Him; i.e. concentrate on Him; think of Him, dedicate all your work to Him!

Avar tyag tu tisay chitar…

When I was a school-boy growing up in Karachi, a holy man visited the city. I often went to sit at his feet and listen to his teachings. Once when I took leave of him, I said to him, "Baba, please give me a teaching."

Do you know what he said to me? He said, "*Sher bano, kutta nahi bano.*" Be a lion don't be a dog.

I was thoroughly bewildered. I said to him hesitantly, "Baba, I think I am a lion, because I was born under the sign of Leo. But what do you mean by saying don't be a dog?"

The holy man explained, "If you throw a ball at a dog, what does the dog do? It runs after the ball! If you throw anything at a lion, he will ignore that object and go after you. He will go after the thrower, not the object that is thrown."

We are all the time thinking about what has been thrown at us; about circumstances and conditions in which we live, about the changing vicissitudes of life, the passing shows of life. We do not think of Him, the Thrower who has thrown all these things at us!

If you wish to think of Him, you must empty your mind of all else. So long as you hold worries and anxieties in the mind, so long as your mind is not empty you cannot think of Him —and you will not be at peace. Therefore, empty your mind of all worries and anxiety. Be like the lion, not like the dog!

Que sera, sera! *Whatever will be, will be!* So why worry?

But it is not enough to succumb to fatalism and say, "I can't change what is to happen." I would like you to go one step further and say, "Whatever happened, whatever is happening, whatever will happen is all for the best." We need to assert again and again, that there is a meaning of mercy in all that happens to us. All experiences in life come to teach us something. We must accept it as a blessing—and we will be abundantly blessed.

Instead of worrying, let us turn to God in prayer and place all our burdens at His Lotus feet. This will give us an immediate feeling of peace and relaxation, enabling us to tackle the problems and perplexities of life in a spirit of calm surrender.

Why should we carry heavy burdens on our minds and hearts, when we can easily cast our burdens at the feet of Him who is strong enough to bear all the burdens of all the worlds?

Therefore, empty your mind of all worry and anxiety. Cast your burdens at His feet and He will give you the calmness, courage and confidence to face the challenges of life!

Step 4: Don't Concentrate on Problems—Concentrate on Solutions

There was a professor of economics who was discussing the theory of demand and supply with his students. At the end of the session, he asked the students, "Can you name anything—any product or service—of which the supply always exceeds the demand?"

Even before the others could apply their minds to the question, one student shot up like an arrow and said, "Sir, I can tell you one thing of which the supply always exceeds the demand. That thing is 'PROBLEMS'. Their supply is unlimited, even when our demand for them is NIL."

He was right, wasn't he? The pathways of our life seem to be strewn with problems and challenges. There is hardly a day when we do not handle some problem or the other. It is as if they are waiting in a never-ending queue outside your door; barely have you handled one problem when another immediately rears its head.

Kumar and Reena are a happily married couple. Kumar is a successful young entrepreneur, while Reena has always been a homemaker. They have two beautiful children, a lovely apartment in Mumbai, with servants to attend to the household chores.

The tightening of the money supply prior to the annual budget was beginning to affect Kumar's business adversely. Suddenly the banks seemed to tighten their fists and all his ambitious expansion plans had to be put on hold. One evening he returned home, mentally exhausted, after a long day of futile meetings with several bank managers. His accountant had warned him that payments to their foreign supplier were overdue. The building contractor who was constructing his new office had asked for more funds. The electricity and telephone bills for the office had arrived—and they were astronomical. Kumar was at the end of his tether, as they say.

As he sank into his armchair wearily, Reena brought him his favorite drink—iced lemon tea. Taking the glass from her, he sighed and remarked, "How calm and peaceful the house is! How I envy you cozily ensconced here all day, unhurried, unhassled, without a care in the world!"

Reena's whole demeanor changed. "How can you be so thoughtless, insensitive and cruel?" she burst out. "Have you any idea how tough it is to run a home? You and the children take everything for granted. Did you know that we have had no water supply throughout the day? Pintu hit a boy on the playground, and he has been suspended from the football team! Priya is down with the measles and the cook wants to go to his village because his mother is ill. And you think I'm calm and relaxed and peaceful here at home? Why don't you stay here—calm and quiet and peaceful—while I run the business?"

Problems are a mark of life; problems are a sign of life. If you ever have a day when you did not have to face a single problem, you will be well advised to read the obituary columns of your newspaper to find out if your name appears there. It is only the dead who don't face problems!

Problems do not come to us by accident. They are deliberately thrown in our way by a beneficent Providence for our own good. In the measure in which we handle these problems successfully, in that measure we will be able to unfold the tremendous powers of the Spirit, the immense energies of the eternal that lie locked up within everyone of us. If we are able to unfold even a fraction of these infinite powers, we would realize that there is nothing that we cannot achieve! And the best way to unfold, unlock these hidden powers is the way of handling problems and challenges in the right way.

What is the right way to handle problems, you may ask. I will tell you: Don't look at the problem, look at the solution! The greatest satisfaction in life comes to you not in running away from problems; not in the dereliction of tough duties—but in meeting and solving problems, in facing up to challenges as a dependable, responsible individual.

Problems do not take you to a dead end. They don't always lead you to a permanent deadlock. Problems are not stumbling blocks, but stepping stones to a richer and more beautiful life. If I may say so, problems are opportunities presented to you. It was a wise man who remarked: "Each problem has hidden in it an opportunity so powerful that it literally dwarfs the problem. The greatest success stories were created by people who recognized a problem and turned it into an opportunity!"

Take a look at the algebra, geometry and mathematics textbooks, which children use in schools. In these books are printed hundreds of 'problems'—chapter after chapter of problems, but in the last few pages of the book are given the answers to those problems. If there are problems there have to be answers too. If a problem has no answer, no solution, it will not be given to you! In other words, there can be no problem which is insoluble.

The Gita tells us that our life is based on *dwandas*— binary opposites. You see these pairs of opposites everywhere around you. Light and darkness, night and day, heat and cold, loss and gain, pain and pleasure, in and out, up and down, far and near, good and evil; praise and censure – the list is endless. You cannot have one without the other, can you? Can there be day without night or pleasure without pain? Can you come down without going up? These pairs of opposites are like the two sides of a coin. You cannot know what heat is unless you feel cold. You cannot know what light is without darkness. So it is with problems! Whenever you have a problem, you must have a solution—a solution which is contained within the problem!

Problems are there for all of us; everyone has got to face them. Some of us have health problems; some of us have relationship problems; many people face financial problems; others have problems of personal adjustment. On a large scale there are diplomatic problems, and so on.

Everyone of us has to face his or her own problems— and without exception, each of us is apt to imagine that *our* problem is the worst of all.

A little girl was taken to an ENT specialist, as she was suffering from an ear infection. As the doctor was examining her, she said to him, "Doctor, I've got the *worst* earache in the world!" The doctor smiled and said to her, "Tell me, my child, what makes you to feel that your earache is the worst in the world? Isn't that a little too much?" The girl replied, "Of course not, doctor! It is the worst earache because it is *my* earache!"

Too true! Because it is my problem it is the worst in the world! But I repeat: Every problem has a solution. There is no problem that is insoluble.

Sometime ago, when I was aboard a plane, my attention was drawn to the wings of the Boeing aircraft and I saw a number of blades extending across the wings. I was told th   hese blades were called voltage generators. Their function was to create turbulence, to create roughness, so that the aircraft could be steered with accuracy. If the going were very smooth, I was told, there could not be accurate steering. Roughness and turbulence were essential so that the aircraft could keep to its flight path. Likewise, if we had a very smooth sailing through life, if we had no problems, we may lose our sense of direction! Life without problems would be dull, static, and uninteresting! After all, what is man without his fighting spirit and the determination to surmount obstacles and achieve his goals?

May be it is that we are all becoming 'soft', living in this push-button age. There is a gadget for everything now. All you have to do is push a button, and things happen automatically. We are living very easy, comfortable lives, compared to our ancestors—this is why we are daunted by problems.

It is said that there are three ways of meeting a problem: but only *one* of them is the right way. What are those three ways?

The first way is the way of avoidance. You avoid the problem. You run away from it. The approach of the problem unnerves you—and you choose the way of escape.

There are some students who are afraid to face tests and examinations. Whenever class test is announced, they simply stay away. But of course, they cannot avoid the annual examination. If they do not pass this examination, they cannot pass—they cannot be promoted to a higher class. Then it is that they realize, that all those class tests were meant to help them pass this crucial final exam.

When you avoid a problem, when you run away from it, you may be sure that it will return to you sooner or later. Repeated avoidance will only make the problem really formidable—and you cannot escape it any more!

May I share with you an unforgettable experience from my boyhood? When I was a student in primary school, there was a vendor of sweets who stood outside the school building, and invited children to play a gambling game. It was very simple. You threw dice and if you got the right number, you won extra sweets. If you didn't get the right number, you had to pay him money.

The sweets he sold, known as *gubeet*, were very popular among the children, and I am afraid many of us succumbed to the temptation.

Initially, when I started this 'gamble', I won. They call it beginners luck, don't they? So I won —and I was thrilled! And I was tempted to play again and again, when I started to lose. Would you believe it, in a matter of minutes I lost fourteen *annas!* In those days, it was an astronomical sum for a little boy. We used to receive one *paisa*—a fraction of an *anna* as pocket money. How I managed to lose fourteen *annas* was something I simply could not figure!

The sweet vendor was a tall and hefty *pathan* who was not to be trifled with. Initially, I requested him to give me a little time to pay him the amount that I had lost. He agreed, but warned me that he would always keep an eye on me.

Days passed by, and I simply could not muster the required amount. As for the *pathan*, his patience was exhausted and he began to threaten me. I was unnerved, and I sought every means I could to avoid him. If I saw him at a distance, I would slip away through a nearby alley.

Of course, he caught up with me. One day, as I turned the corner of a lane, there he stood, towering over me. He caught me by the collar and demanded his money.

The truth dawned on me, that I could never, ever run away from my problems—especially, if those problems were the consequences of my own actions. I had tried to avoid my problem, and it had only become more menacing!

My 'debt' was paid in *painful* installments—but the lesson was not to be forgotten! I still remember the towering *pathan* wielding a stick in his hand. If you avoid a problem, you may escape for a short while, but it will come back to you with a stick in its hand! It will confront you and say to you, "If you do not accept the message I have brought for you, if you do not learn the lesson that I have come to teach you, I will have to deal with you in a hard way!"

Never avoid a problem! You cannot solve a problem by running away from it! If you do, it will come back to you, it will come back to you with a vengeance!

The way of avoidance is the way of folly. The more you try to avoid it, the more formidable it becomes, until you realize you cannot come out of it!

The second way—another wrong way—of meeting a problem is the way of passive resignation. Many people adopt this as a 'default' approach. Their typical reaction is: What cannot be cured must be endured. "What can we do!" they exclaim. "We have to face this problem. There is no escape."

This is also a negative approach. You may actually tackle the problem in one way or the other —but it is not likely to be the best way. It may be marginally better than the way of avoidance —but it is not the ideal way.

There is a third way of facing problems—the right way, what I call the way of victory. This is the way of *glad acceptance*. Move forward to greet the problem with the words, "I welcome you! Tell me what message do you bring to me from God?"

Some of you who read this are likely to exclaim: "It is all very well for Dada to say we must welcome problems, and greet them as our friends! What does he know about the difficulties we face, the hassles we undergo, and the tension they cause"?

Believe me friends, I *do* understand! Life is not given to us on easy terms. Life *is* strewn with difficulties, dangers, trials and tribulations. All I wish to say that they are given to us by God *for our own good!* Life is a school—it is not a pleasure-hunting ground where we seek sense gratification. Life is a school, and experience is our teacher. And every experience that comes to us has a valuable lesson to teach us—a lesson that we need to learn. I have come here to the earth to attend the school of life and learn certain lessons. You may have come here to learn certain other lessons. This is why each one of us receives a different set of experiences— to teach us those lessons that are vital for our growth towards perfection. If we fail to learn these lessons – we will be like the cowardly schoolboy who could not take his exams, and therefore, could not be promoted to a higher class!

Let me share with you, this parable that tells us another way to look at problems.

God, before He sent His children down to the earth, gave each of them a carefully selected package of problems. He said to each child, with a smile, "These are yours, and yours alone. These problems bring with them very special blessings—and only *you* have the special talents and abilities to make these problems your servants."

God added softly, "Now go down to earth. Know that I love you beyond measure. The problems I give you are a symbol of that love. The monument you make of your life with the help of your problems will be a symbol of your love for Me, your Heavenly Father. Go in peace— and be blessed!"

Therefore, I say to you dear friends: Move forward to greet every problem when it appears on your horizon! Don't be frightened; don't run away from it. Meet it, face it bravely and actually co-operate with it, knowing that it brings to you a rich treasure, a treasure which you must receive! This is a right way of meeting a problem. It is the way of acceptance, the way of victory!

When I was about eight years old, a family friend brought me two packets on my birthday. He said to me, "I have brought you a birthday gift – but you will have to choose one of these packets."

I looked at the two packets. One of them was wrapped in shiny, glossy gift—paper, and tied up neatly with a red ribbon. The other was wrapped up in an old, shabby newspaper and looked quite unattractive.

My first impulse, naturally, was to pick up the glossy packet. But a voice within me said, "No! This is not the one meant for you. Choose the other one!"

I obeyed the voice instinctively, and I chose the shabby packet. And the gentleman patted me one the shoulder and said, "You have chosen right!"

I opened the packet and I couldn't believe my eyes! It was a Conklin pen – the very thing that I longed to have, for days, weeks, even months together! Today, you have Parker, Sheafers, Mont Blanc pens—in those days, Conklin was the best fountain pen available. The packet which was dirty, shabby, soiled on the outside, had a rich treasure inside! And the gentleman said to me, "The shiny glossy packet only has an ordinary lead pencil inside. You were smart to choose the shabby packet!"

Problems too, are like gifts that come wrapped in shabby parcels. Do not be put off by their rough and rude exterior—for they contain valuable gifts!

Even as there are three ways of meeting a problem, there are three ways in which you can view a problem; three windows through which you gaze at the problem. These are the windows of time, space and eternity.

Time is a dimension that changes the way you look at things. A little girl of six worries about her dolls, her ribbons and her dresses; a teenager worries about her complexion, her nails and the pimples on her face. A young woman worries about her job, her future prospects—about the man she is going to marry! The young mother worries about her children and about her household chores. A grandmother wishes above all, to see her grandchildren married and settled! If you tell your grandmother that you are upset about your pimple, she would laugh out loud!

Go back in time, and think of the problems you faced 10 or 15 years ago. I dare say you will find it difficult even to recall them! They may have given you sleepless nights then, but are all forgotten now!

Today, you may be facing what seems to be a tough problem. But if you go forward ten or fifteen years, you will realize that this problem appears so insignificant.

There is another window through which you can gaze at your problem—and that is the window of space. Problems that you face in a particular place will disappear when you move on from that place—it may be an organization in which you are working, or an area in which you live now. When you move away from that place, many problems are simply left behind!

The third window through which you can look at a problem is the window of eternity. Our life on earth is brief, finite—but our life in eternity is endless. Alas, we are so identified with the body that we fail to perceive the life of the Spirit that transcends our life on earth. We have a future that stretches far into eternity.

Our life on this earth plane is but a moment in eternity. When we learn to view our problems through the windows of eternity, we will find they are so trivial, so tiny, that they do not affect us at all!

When problems surface, insights disappear. When insights surface, problems disappear!

Step 5: Count Your Blessings

A few years ago, when I was in the U.S. I gave a talk on "How to make problems work for you." On the very next day, a brother wrote to me, "I am on a gloomy express train carrying an excess of negative baggage. What can I do to get off this grouchy track?"

Then and there I put down a few words on paper—I wrote a small poem which I would like to pass on to you. There is not much of music or imagery in it, but I do believe that if we all follow the teaching it has to offer, it will be to our advantage:

> When all is dark as a starless night
> And there's not a ray of hope in sight
> Then count your blessings one by one
> You will be amazed at all that God has done!

When we are feeling slightly ill, just a little feverish, we rush to the medicine cabinet. At the slightest hint of a headache, we go in search of Advil or Paracetamol. At the least hint of acidity, we keep Pepcid or Digene handy. But when the mind is upset, when the mind is sick with worry, anxiety and negative thinking, we do nothing! We just wallow in our misery, we allow ourselves to suffer "on the gloomy express", with our "excess negative baggage", as my friend put it so picturesquely!

Let me offer you a prescription for an 'upset mind.' It is a prescription you can write out for yourself! Just take a sheet of paper and write on it all the things for which you are grateful to God.

When I offer this suggestion to my friends, many of them respond, "What have I got to be thankful for? Nothing!"

Do you know the value of your eyes? Do you know the value of your ears? Your hands? Your feet? Your mind? Your family and friends? If someone were to offer you a million dollars, would you give away your eyes?

I often narrate to my friends the story of the rich young maiden who fell in love with a wonderful young man. I don't know why we say *fell* in love because true love can really lift you up! But be as it may, this rich young girl fell in love with this wonderful boy, and she sought her father's permission to marry him. The father was particular only about one thing: "As long as the young man is rich enough to take care of your needs, I have no objection to your marrying him."

But that was just the trouble. The young man had everything a girl would want—except money!

The girl went to meet the family solicitor, who was also her godfather, and loved her dearly. "He is the only one for me," she said to the solicitor. "I don't care for money—it comes and goes. You must help me to convince daddy that this is the right match for me."

The solicitor asked her to bring the young man to meet him. Having spoken to him, he was convinced that the girl had indeed made a wise choice. The only problem now would be to convince the father that the young man was 'rich' enough to suit his pride.

The solicitor looked at the young man in the eye and said, "Will you give away one of your eyes if I offered you a million rupees?"

The young man stared at him, horrified. "Of course not," he said, shocked. "I'm in love with this girl, and I would like to look at her all my life, with *both* my eyes. You can keep your million rupees."

"Alright then," continued the solicitor. "I will offer you two million! Will you give away one of your eyes? After all, you still have the other!"

"Why don't you understand?" snapped the young man in exasperation. "I'm not in business of organ selling to raise funds. What do you take me for?"

"That may not be so," persisted the lawyer. "But just think of the advantage you will have with two million in your bank account! You can become an entrepreneur! You will get a head start over others."

"Let me tell you something Sir," said the young man patiently. "I am hard working, intelligent and very well qualified. In a couple of months, when I step out of my university, the best companies will be ready to hire me! I can make two million—perhaps even three million—in a couple of years. I would be a fool to part with my precious eyes for the sake of a little money like that!"

"Do you mean to say you refuse an offer of two million for just one of your eyes?"

"Sir, forgive me, I think you are just wasting my time and yours."

"Thank you, dear chap," said the solicitor warmly. "You've told me all I wanted to know."

Turning to the girl he said, "You can leave your father to me now; I can convince him to give you permission to marry the man of your choice."

That evening, the solicitor met the father of the girl. He brought up the subject of his daughter's marriage. "All I want is that he is rich enough to be my son-in-law," the father repeated.

"I don't know what you mean by 'rich enough,'" said the lawyer. "All I know is he's got two prime possessions, for one of which he was offered rupees two million just this morning. But he refused to part with it."

"Oh?" said the father, startled. "Is that so? Then he must be worth at least four million! In that case, he can certainly marry my daughter!"

Should we not feel grateful to God for the gifts He has bestowed on us—two eyes with which to see the beauty of the world around us, two ears with which to hear music, song, conversation and children's laughter; two hands with which to do a thousand things; two feet which can take us wherever we choose to walk!

And that is not all. He has given us people who love us—family, brothers and sisters, friends and well-wishers!

> Count your blessings instead of your crosses
> Count your gains instead of your losses
> Count your joys instead of your woes
> Count your friends instead of your foes
> Count your smiles instead of your tears
> Count your courage instead of your fears
> Count your full years instead of your lean
> Count your kind deeds instead of your mean
> Count your health instead of your wealth
> Love the world as much as you love yourself
> Count your blessings!

It is so easy to feel sorry for oneself, but we must realize that we take a lot of things for granted.

• You can read and write, which sets you apart from millions of people who are still illiterate.

• If you can use a computer—if you possess a PC— you are luckier than billions of people who are not so lucky!

• Think of the comfortable clothes you are wearing— think of the choice you can exercise, deciding what to wear each day.

• Think of the food you eat—the preferences you have—the likes and dislikes you insist upon: "no cabbage, no spinach, no brinjals!"

Psychiatrists actually make an exercise out of this. They recommend that you sit with a few glossy magazines, a pair of scissors and a glue stick. Now, they tell you to snip out, cut out words, phrases and pictures which remind you of your blessings. You are then required to paste all of these on a chart paper, as a sort of, 'collage of blessings' and put it up at a prominent place to remind you of your countless blessings!

I assure you, even if you were to spend a whole day making a list of your blessings, you will find that there are quite a few that you have overlooked. I know of a sister who made a comprehensive list, only to realize she had left out so many of her favorite things—her pet dog, her preferred brand of coffee, the song (and the singer) which always lifted her spirit, her favorite novel, her faithful domestic servant, her comfortable walking shoes and so on and so forth. There seemed to be practically no end to the number of things for which she owed gratitude to God!

When you become aware of 'abundance' in your own life, your attitude to circumstances will change and you will be ready to take on 'lean' and 'dark' days with a more positive and constructive attitude. This sense of 'abundance' will add to your faith and contribute to your peace of mind.

When I talk about 'abundance,' let me make it clear, I do not refer merely to material wealth. I am not at all sure that 'money' is the most valuable thing in our lives. I am reminded of the words of Alan Gregg: "The human race has had a long experience and a fine tradition in surviving adversity. But we now face a task for which we have very little experience—the task of surviving prosperity."

A lady was shopping for her weekly groceries at a huge super market in New York. In about twenty minutes, her shopping trolley was full to the brim, with all the stuff that she needed, and all the items on her list had been neatly ticked off. As she was about to reach the cash—counter, she remembered that she wanted to pick up bananas. Promptly, she retraced her steps to the 'fruits' section, only to discover that the store was out of bananas that day!

For a minute or so, she was annoyed and vexed. How could the store authorities be so inefficient and incompetent as not to stock what the customers needed! After all, it was only bananas she wanted, not Kiwi or passion fruit or some such exotic delicacy. As she stared straight ahead, frowning, her eyes caught the scene outside—it was December, and there was snow falling.

The lady stopped in her tracks. This was New York and no bananas grew in the vicinity. The bananas her family ate every week, were imported from warmer climes, and sold for a few dollars at every supermarket, but she had just taken them for granted. After all, it was *only* bananas! But today, when she had thought of making banana milkshake as a special treat for the family, bananas were missing from the super market shelf. Like so many other things in life—like the dozens of items in her shopping trolley at this very moment—she had simply taken them for granted! She then realized to instead be grateful for all the other stock of items and fruits which were stacked up in her trolley.

"How can I count my blessings when my alarm rings at 5:30a.m?" asked someone I know.

True, people tend to shut their eyes tight and clutch their blankets when the alarm goes off. But they will do well to thank God that they can hear—for there are many who are deaf!

We would all do well to spend at least ten minutes everyday, appreciating all the things and people we take for granted—your favorite armchair, your cozy bed, the book you enjoyed reading, the goodies that come out from your kitchen, the view from your window, the hot water, the familiar living space and a hundred other things without which your home would not be a home at all! Think of all the ways in which you use the space and the objects; think of how much you enjoy using them; think of what you will do *without* them … how different, how strange your life would be without them!

The truth is we regard a lot of things we own as merely 'utility' items. A pen, a pencil, a calculator, a computer, even a motorcar, is all necessary for us; we do not regard them as worthy of appreciation.

True, each of these has its use. But unless you learn to appreciate their utility, you will not really value them! And it is only when you value them that they give you real satisfaction.

A friend told me about a cartoon that he came across in the Sunday magazine section of his newspaper:

A working couple is musing over a romantic movie which they have just seen on TV. The husband sighs.

"I wonder if there is really such a thing as a *fairytale romance*!"

"Of course there is," says the wife. "Ours is a fairytale romance, isn't it?"

"Oh, you think so? Then why aren't we living *happily ever after*?"

"But we *are*," the wife insists.

"Can anyone be happy while they are slogging six days a week at a boring job, paying a mortgage and trying to save for a holiday? Cinderella and Prince Charming did not have to pay bills and balance their checkbooks!"

"Well, they didn't have indoor plumbing, electricity and cable TV either," the wife says.

She was one who knew how to count her blessings!

The trouble with most of us is that we are so busy chasing after more—more money, more comforts, more opportunities—that we fail to appreciate what we *have* already!

- Do you have a family?
- Do you get safe drinking water?
- Do you get two/three meals a day?
- Do you have a college degree?
- Do you have friends?
- Do you have a home to live in?

And finally, do you know there are hundreds of thousands of people who will answer 'NO' to all these questions?

Becoming aware of your blessings, listing them, counting them and appreciating them has a positive effect on your attitude and thinking.

Researchers at an American University asked a set of college students to keep a daily journal. Half of them were told to record all the things which they appreciated and felt grateful for. The other half were told to note down all the hassles and difficulties they had to face everyday.

After a month of journal entries, it was found that the gratitude group felt 'on top of the world'. They hardly had any illnesses or complaints to report. What is more, they felt that they could offer emotional support and help to others who were not so lucky!

Here is a message that was circulated on the Internet:

If you woke up this morning with more health than illness—thank God! You are luckier than the million or so people who did not survive last week.

If you have never been exposed to the horrors of war, the solitude of prison, the loneliness of exile or the pangs of starvation—thank God! You are better off then 500 million people in the world, who have had to face these horrors!

If you can go to your church or temple or synagogue without fear of harassment—thank God! There are three billion people in the world who do not have freedom of worship.

If you have food in the refrigerator, change of clothes to wear, a roof over your head and a place to sleep—thank God! You are better off than 75% of the world's population.

If you have a bank account with some savings, money in your wallet and a little cash to spare at home—thank God! You are among the top 10 percent the world's wealthy people!

Count your blessings! And you will be filled with hope, optimism and faith that will help you face the challenges of life!

Step 6: Accept God's Will

May I pass on to you a *mantra* which is sure to bring you peace? It is a prayer which a saint, a holy man of God used to offer again and again. Inscribe it on the tablet of your heart. Repeat it again and again—remember it by day and night, for it is really simple:

> Yes Father, Yes Father—Yes and always yes!
> Yes Father, Yes Father—Yes and always yes!

There are people who are upset with me because I advocate the philosophy of acceptance. They say to me, that this will make people lazy and lethargic; they will give up all their drive and ambition and simply sink into passive resignation.

I beg to differ! People who believe in the supremacy of the Almighty, people who learn to accept His Divine Will, never ever give in to lethargy and pessimism. They do as the Lord bids them in the Gita—they put in their best efforts; they do not slacken; they do their best to achieve what they want. But if they do not achieve the desired results, they do not give in to despair and frustration; they do not give in to disappointment.

An inspector of schools visited our Mira School in Pune. During an interaction with the students, he asked them, "Tell me where is Pune situated?" Many hands shot up, and the children gave the answer in chorus, "In the State of Maharashtra."

"Where is Maharashtra?" the inspector persisted.

"In India," said the children.

"And where is India?"

"In Asia".

"Can you tell me where is Asia?"

"In the world."

"And where is the world?"

A pregnant silence prevailed. But one little girl came out with a sterling answer. "Sir, the world is safe in the Hands of God!"

The world is safe in the hands of God! Why then should we lose our sleep and peace of mind?

There are so many situations and circumstances in life that shatter our peace. But how long can we allow ourselves to wallow in sorrow and self-pity? The call of life is Onward, Forward, Godward! Men may come and men may go, but life goes on forever! Lives may come to an end, but life on earth must go on!

"Would you know who is the greatest saint in the world?" asks William Law. "It is not he who prays most or fasts most; it is not he who gives most alms or is most eminent for temperance, charity or justice; but it is he who is always thankful to God; who wills everything God wills, who receives everything as an instance of God's goodness and has a heart always ready to praise God for it."

It is said that the Pilgrim Fathers—the early European settlers in America— "made seven times more graves than huts." That is, hundreds of them lost their lives, while only a handful survived, but at the cost of losing their near and dear ones. Thus their settlements had "more graves than huts." And yet, they set aside a special day for Thanksgiving! They knew what it is to accept the will of God!

Yes Father—Yes and always Yes!

Acceptance in the spirit of gratitude unlocks the fullness in our lives. It can turn despair into faith, strife into harmony, chaos into order, and confusion into clear understanding. It restores peace into our hearts and helps us to look forward to the morrow in the faith that God is always with us!

It is not enough to speak of gratitude or enact deeds of gratitude—we must *live* gratitude by practicing acceptance of God's will in all conditions, in all incidents and accidents of life.

When things are not going as we wish, we tend to develop 'tunnel vision'—that is, focus on the dark, negative side of life. However, we will do well to remember that it is always darkest before dawn and trial and adversity can be powerful agents of change that help us grow, evolve to become better human beings, and eventually make a success of our lives.

There are several things in our lives about which we are not happy. Our 'wish list' for something different, something more, something other than what we possess extends to several aspects of our daily life.

Many affluent teenagers now carry cell phones—something unheard of even ten years ago. But not all of them are happy with these gadgets. Every six months or so, they wish to change models; they want more 'features'; they want the latest. When they are denied what they are want, they sulk, they grumble, they wish they had richer and kinder parents.

Homemakers, mothers and wives wish to have better equipped kitchens; they want more gadgets, more equipment, more aids to make their life easy. They want better furniture, more expensive curtains, and nicer clothes to wear. Men want a better job, a better boss, a bigger car, more money and more leisure.

There's nothing wrong in wishing for any of these things. The problem arises when we develop a feeling of active discontent with what we are and what we have. Discontent leads to depression, and depression destroys our peace of mind.

A psychiatrist has described depression as "anger turned inward." We are angry with so many things and so many people; we are discontented with the way we live our lives—and we are angry with ourselves.

If we persist with depression, discontent and anger, it will not be long before we start blaming God for all the ills that beset us!

- God could have made me taller, slimmer, more beautiful.
- God could have given me more money, a richer husband, a more understanding wife, kinder parents, better friends.
- God could have made my children more intelligent, more accomplished, more obedient, more appreciative…

The list is endless!

So the blame shifts to God! Are we not accusing Him of being unfair, unjust, and unkind when we perceive our life to be all wrong? In the end it all turns out to be His fault!

Patience and acceptance are difficult to cultivate. Without them, there can be no inner development, no spiritual growth.

That is not at all! When we lack the wisdom to accept God's will, we cause ourselves a lot of unnecessary grief; grief that arises because reality differs from our wishes and our plans.

Giving up *our* will and accepting God's will can involve some painful losses.

This incident happened to a student at one of our institutions. Waiting at a bus stop after college, she began to talk to her friends on her mobile phone. As she was making the third call, the bus arrived. Hastily she cut the call, put the cell phone into her tote bag and climbed onto the bus.

Barely a few minutes later, she felt her cell phone was missing. She checked her bag and found that it was indeed gone! She raised an alarm, got off the bus even before it reached the next stop, and retraced her way back to the bus stop, hoping against hope that her cell phone might be lying around somewhere.

Her friend, who had accompanied her, urged her to return home, but the girl would not do it! She insisted on talking to the people at the bus stop, asking them if they had seen anyone suspicious, noticed anything unusual … all to no avail.

Two hours later, she returned home, angry, hurt and miserable. She would not eat lunch; she would not talk to her mother.

People lose their cell phones; people lose their wallets and credit cards; but life cannot come to a stop because you have lost something. How long will you worry, how long will you complain, feel bitter and be miserable?

It was St. Francis who prayed, "Lord give me the strength to change the things I can change, patience to accept the things I cannot change, and wisdom to know the difference."

Wisdom consists in accepting what you cannot change. What cannot be cured must be endured. This is not passive resignation or pessimistic self-denial. It is the way of wisdom which leads to peace.

We need to grow in the spirit of acceptance, for life is full of unexpected events. A dear one is suddenly snatched away from us. Initially, we are devastated; we weep, we shed bitter tears; we refuse to eat, we cannot sleep.

That is but natural, you might say. But how long can you go on? Will weeping, fasting and vigil bring back your loved one to life?

And then again, aren't we all mortal? Can we determine the length and duration of our own life—or anyone else's life?

Wisdom consists in accepting God's will—not with despair or resignation, but in peace and faith, knowing that our journey through life has been perfectly planned by Infinite love and Infinite wisdom. There can be no mistake in God's plan for us!

Again and again, we try to run away from difficult situations; again and again we rebel, react with anger and bitterness. How can we ever be at peace?

The answer is simple: Grow in the spirit of surrender to God; develop the spirit of acceptance. "Not my will, but Thy will be done, O Lord!" this must be the constant utterance on your lips.

To seek refuge is to trust the Lord—fully, completely, entirely. It is to know that He is the one Light that we need in the darkest hours of our life. He is the all-loving One whose ears are ever attentive to the prayers of His wayward children. He is the all-knowing One who does the very best for us. With Him, all things are possible: and if He chooses *not* to do certain things for us which we want Him to do, it is not because He cannot do them, but because He knows better—he knows we require something else for our own good.

So it is that He who has taken refuge in the Lord is ever at peace. "Not my will, but Thy will be done, O Lord," he prays. Whatever happens, "I accept! I accept! I accept!" is his *mantra*. "Yes Father, Yes and always Yes!" is his response to all incidents and all accidents of life. Nothing—no accident, no loss, no tragedy—can disturb his equanimity.

Step 7: Do Your Best — Leave The Rest To God!

We have seen that desire is the root cause of all suffering. Our expectations, which are not always realistic, often lead to disappointment and frustration. Are we then to live without hope, without aspirations?

The answer is a resounding NO!

Work is worship—and *karma*, or action, is unavoidable for those who are born on this earth. But the secret of inner peace is to work without attachment to the results.

The laws of nature drive all of us to activity, for we cannot survive without action. But the wise ones act without attachment—with detachment—without looking for results. Success and failure do not influence their attitude to their duty.

Of course, some of you are bound to ask, "Is it really possible for us to act without desiring any kind of results?"

In the *Bhagavad Gita*, Sri Krishna has given us not one, not two, but three strong motives which should guide all our actions:

1. Duty—for the sake of duty.
2. Work—for the sake of inner purification.
3. Action—an offering to the Lord.

In fact, the Lord even goes on to tell Arjuna that desireless action is actually better than renunciation of action.

There are people who are constantly chasing 'goals' and 'targets'—more money, a better job, higher pay, and greater satisfaction.

Yet others grumble and complain all the time, because they feel their work is unrecognized, unrewarded, unappreciated.

How may we avoid such disappointment, frustration and this restless drive?

Simply by surrendering the fruits of action to the Lord! Let us stop chasing after 'personal satisfaction' and 'individual happiness.' Let us make our work—all our work—an offering to the Lord.

Do your best—but leave the rest to God! When you allow yourself to become an instrument of God, you will find that you can actually work better, and achieve greater success—for you will be freed from your own personal limitations.

When you rid yourself of the desire to 'achieve' results, when you are free from anxiety and stress that arises from expectations, you escape the twin perils of egoistic arrogance on one hand, and dejection/depression on the other. If your efforts are crowned with success, it is His doing; if you should face failure, it is His will!

In this way you are really putting into practice the maxim—work is worship. Your work becomes an act of devotion—and when it is performed in this spirit, work will always be a wonderful, pleasant experience for you!

We read of Jesus that he got into the boat of Simon Peter and bade him row out to the middle of the Sea of Galilee and cast his net for fish.

Peter hesitated; for he and his mates had spent a frustrating day trying to catch fish in vain. Perhaps they were hungry and tired, and could not wait to get home. Nevertheless, he did as Jesus asked him to do—and the Bible tells us that his boat literally overflowed with the catch, and his mates had to be called in to help with the load, and their boats too were fully laden!

The point is that Peter did not tell Jesus, "Sorry, I don't want to try again. I'm frustrated enough as it is." He set aside his disappointment and weariness and did what he was told to do.

You do not have to struggle; you do not have to fear and be anxious; you only have to allow yourself to become an instrument of God's Will—and the Divine Plan will be revealed to you and through you.

Avoid overwork! For it has been the graveyard of many a noble soul. The overworked man is a burden to himself and a nuisance to others. Do not rush through your daily tasks. Move slowly and quietly from one work to another, pausing again and again, for a brief while, to remember the Lord, to offer a little prayer, before you continue with your work.

It is not the *amount* of work we do that matters, but the *way* we do it; it is not *what* we do, but *how* we do it. There are many people who toil and drudge and slave, day after day, month after month, year after year—and their work is but a shadow on the wall. It vanishes the moment it is born. True work, abiding work, the work that transforms lives, flows out of the centre within the heart; the centre of harmony and happiness, peace and joy.

When you work in this spirit, you will find that you are freed from all care for the morrow, all fear of the future! What will happen to me tomorrow? Who will feed my family? Who will supply my daily needs? All these thoughts will cease to trouble you—for you know that the Lord will provide. It is His sole responsibility to take care of us and look after all our needs.

Convert your work into *yagna*—an offering and you are linked with the Lord. But remember, you must offer Him nothing but the best that you are capable of! The light shines in your life when you connect yourself with the Great Light: a new power, a new *shakti* will course through your veins, and you will find that God never fails you!

The majority of men have their families to look after, bills to pay and a livelihood to earn. They have to provide for their children's education, pay taxes and utility bills. In these days of increasing costs, they find it difficult even to procure the bare necessities of life for themselves and for those who depend on them.

What are they to do?

The essential thing they need is a change of outlook!

As it is, many of us place too much dependence on ourselves, our efforts and endeavors. We keep God out of the picture.

Of course human effort has its place in life. But we need to understand that above all effort is His Will and His Grace. And He is the giver of all that is! So let us learn to work as His agents and He will take care of everything else! We are His children—and when we work to the best of our ability and capability, it will be His responsibility to provide for us and take care of our every need.

He who has surrendered himself to God finds the greatest security of life. He need wander no more. All his cares and burdens are borne by the Lord Himself. In the beautiful words of the *Gita:*

They who worship Me
Depending on Me alone,
Thinking of no other –
They are My sole responsibility!
Their burdens are My burdens;
To them I bring full security!

Step 8: Pray Without Ceasing!

If you would have inner peace, pray without ceasing! This is one spiritual discipline that can go on forever! You cannot sit in mediation very long. You cannot fast longer than a few days. Every other spiritual discipline has its limitations as far as the average man is concerned—but prayer can go on forever!

You will find the following injunction in the Bible:

Be anxious for nothing, but in everything, by prayer and supplication with thanksgiving, let your requests be made known to God. And the peace of God, which surpasses all comprehension, shall guard your hearts and minds …

(Philippions 4: 6-7)

We are actually ordered—indeed commanded—not to worry, not to be anxious, but to pray specially for our requests; pray with thanksgiving. And we are promised that when we do so faithfully, God's peace will guard our hearts. What a wonderful promise this is!

Prayer is a very simple matter. For me, it is just speaking with God. He is with you everywhere: He is available to you at all times. You will never find His line 'busy' or 'engaged.' Reaching Him on the prayer-line is quicker than the 'speed dial' on your cell phone. All you have to do is think of Him, shut out the world momentarily, and start a loving conversation with Him. If you wish, it can go on and on and on!

We waste much of our time in activities of no account. Our mind is so distracted, it keeps running from pillar to post. Why not engage this distracted mind in a loving, intimate conversation with God?

Prayer need not be a complicated affair. Suppose a friend drops in for a visit. Wouldn't it be natural for you to welcome him, discuss your plans, dreams, and aspirations with him? Would you not seek his help and support in all that you do? This is exactly what you must do in your prayers, too—for God is the Friend of all Friends.

It is said that an Emperor asked the Rabbi Joshua: "If God exists why am I not able to see him?" The Rabbi said: "But that is Impossible." The Emperor insisted that he should be able to see God. The Rabbi said to the Emperor, "Are you able to look at the sun? If you cannot look at the sun which is but a servant of God, how can you see God?"

Therefore, do not doubt God's presence or indeed His omnipotence. He is there for you—all you have to do is call upon Him—and He will be there to help you.

Let me remind you of my words repeated earlier:

Thou wilt keep him in perfect peace whose mind is stayed on Thee!

You must remember too, that what is impossible with man is possible with God. Whenever you find yourself in a difficult situation, passing through a period of darkness, there is One who is always there with you. A loved one may be afflicted with an incurable illness—and the doctors give up hope. You are on the verge of bankruptcy—and there is no one you can ask for help. You are in a personal relationship crisis—and the bond seems near breaking point. You have done your very best, but you are unable to solve the problem.

Just hand it over to God!

How can you hand it over to God? Go to Him in prayer. In prayer, place the problem before Him. Tell Him, "Lord, I can do nothing in this matter without you. It is for You to come and help me out."

But remember to *thank* the Lord before you close your prayer. Pray with thanksgiving. Thank the Lord as though He has already answered your prayer. Only remember that His answer may take a while to reach you. Feel that you are well and happy. Feel that your problem has been solved. Allow gratitude to well up in your heart, and you will find that peace fills your mind simultaneously.

What is impossible with man is possible with God! Keep on shooting prayers! People tell me, "Dada, it's alright for you to tell us to pray ceaselessly—but we simply do not have the time!" I say to you, *make* time for prayer. Even as the needle of the compass always points towards the north, our hearts and minds should always turn towards the Lord!

The cure of all ills is contact with God. You may be in dire straits; you may be overwhelmed by problems. But the moment you go within and reach God, nothing can touch you! This is why I urge you again and again, cultivate the habit of prayer, cultivate the habit of daily contact with God. Once you form this habit, it will become such a spontaneous effort, that it will become automatic! You will not have to make any special effort—prayer will come to you naturally. It will just happen! You will think of God all the time—while you walk, while you talk, while you work, He will be the Unseen Presence within you—and you will long for the time when you can be alone with Him, to open out your heart to Him.

It is this longing that we must cultivate though constant prayer. Without this longing, without this yearning, our prayers are shallow and empty; they cannot take us to the depths within. And it is in these depths that God waits for us. When we have learnt to contact Him, it is easy for us to plumb these depths, and hear Him, feel His presence and talk to Him! All this is possible through ceaseless prayer!

"Come unto Me!" says Sri Krishna, "and you will be a direct charge on Me. Your burdens will be My burdens and your joys will be My joys!"

And did not Jesus say, "Seek ye the Kingdom of God and all these things shall be added unto you?"

Seek God—not for material profit, but solely for His love! Peace will not come to us by running after the things which the Earth gives and the Earth takes away. Peace will not come to us by fighting circumstances and struggling against all that happens to us. Peace will come to us when we ourselves enter into the Great Peace of God—through constant prayer.

A young man once said to me, "Dada, I *do* believe in prayer. I do believe that more things are wrought by prayer than this world dreams of. But whenever I turn to God in prayer, I find that a fear grips me. For I am not at all sure what He may do."

So many of us live in this fear! Therefore we are not ready to surrender to His Will. Our 'prayers' in effect, are something like this: "O Lord, who art All-Powerful! Listen to my cry! Rush to my rescue and grant me all that I ask. I want health and happiness. I want bungalows and cars. I want a beautiful, rich wife. I want lots of things that money can buy. I want honor and fame. I want a position of power and authority. I want men to dance in attendance upon me and bow to my every whim. In short, My Lord, I want my will to be done by Thee—and everyone else!"

And so our wish-list increases. Like butterflies, we flit from one sensation to another, in vain search of that lasting peace that will not—cannot—be obtained, until we return to God.

O, traveler, who art weary with thy wanderings. Away from the true Home there is no rest! Return to thy Homeland! And thy Home is God. Remember Him constantly. Pray to Him ceaselessly.

Significant are the words of Sri Krishna in the *Bhagavad Gita:*

> Staying thy haste,
> Do thou stand still in Me!
> United with Me
> Thou wilt attain
> To the Peace
> Of the Eternal –
> The Supreme Bliss
> That abides in Me!

They who are united with the Lord through ceaseless prayer are happy indeed! They have broken the chains of bondage; they are attached to none; the Lord is their sheet-anchor!

In the beginning, you will find that prayer requires discipline and practice. But as time passes, the discipline becomes unnecessary, because prayer becomes a part of your consciousness. After all, prayer is just a concentration of positive thoughts.

Praying ceaselessly is not a ritual; it is not about words or gestures. It has been described as a constant state of awareness of our oneness with God. You may of course, ask for all the good things you need—and you may gain the faith that it is all obtainable to you. For all prayer is effective—but ceaseless prayer has multiplied effect.

A bestselling author and lecturer tells us:

"Never a day goes by when I don't think about God. More than thinking, I experience the presence of God in most of my waking moments. It's a feeling of contentment and satisfaction that's beyond anything that I might convey…"

"Trouble and perplexity drive me to prayer," writes a brother. "And prayer drives away perplexity and trouble."

I would say to him, "Why wait till you are in trouble? Pray ceaselessly ever in the sunshine of happiness! As Walter Muffer observes, "Prayer should not merely be an occasional impulse to which we respond when we are in trouble; prayer is a life attitude."

Let prayer become a way of life with you. Let your every thought, every word, every action, be centered in prayer, as reflected in this ancient Celtic prayer:

> God to enfold me,
> God to surround me,
> God in my speaking,
> God in my thinking.
> God in my sleeping,
> God in my waking,
> God in my watching,
> God in my hoping.
> God in my life,
> God in my lips
> God in my soul,
> God in my heart.
> God in my suffering,
> God in my slumber,
> God in mine ever—living soul
> God in mine eternity.

It was Jesus who said to us, "The Kingdom of God is *within* you." Ceaseless prayer will help you discover that Kingdom and enter within. You identify yourself with your own divinity. Not only do you find inner peace— but you also become empowered to pass it on to others around you. You spread peace, you radiate peace, you share the gift of peace with everyone who comes into contact with you.

I have spoken to you of eight steps to inner peace. These are not the only means, nor are they exhaustive or arbitrary. My intention has been to examine closely, certain important aspects of inner peace. Once we become aware of these aspects, we can take one step at a time, choosing whatever is easiest and appeals most to us. Something tells me, that once we have taken the first few steps, we will walk all the way, all the ways without turning back—for the journey is as peace-filled as the destination!

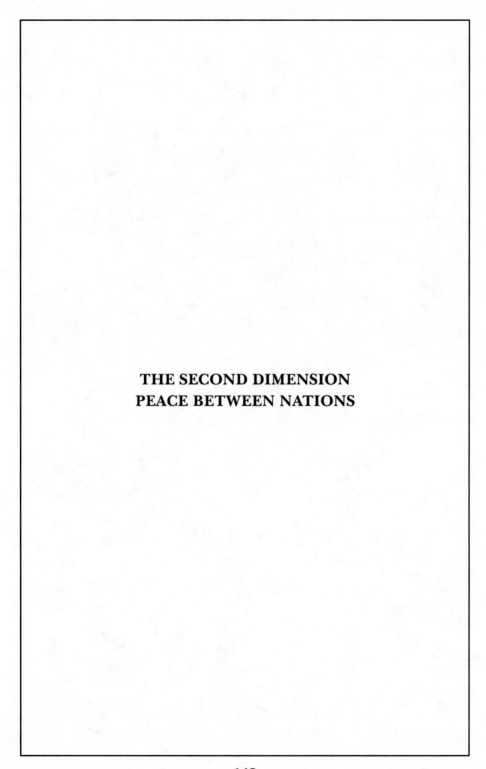

THE SECOND DIMENSION
PEACE BETWEEN NATIONS

Peace between Nations

In one of the early wars fought between England and France, two warships sighted each other from a distance. It was the hour of dawn, and darkness lay upon the sea, like a thick blanket. Thunderclouds flitted across the sky, so that even the stars were hidden from sight. The captain of one ship, spotting another ship at a distance and supposing the other to belong to the enemy, opened a volley of canon fire. It was returned with the same vigor, and a fearful encounter ensured. Both ships were badly damaged, and there were heavy casualties. After about an hour of canon and gunfire, the skies cleared, and in the first glimmer of the morning sun, the sailors discovered to their horror, that both ships were flying an English flag. Quick as the lightning's flash, the fighting ceased abruptly. The ships drew close and exchanged greetings, and grieved sadly over the disastrous mistake.

Don't put this down as a crude mistake made by unsophisticated men in the primitive past. In the 21st century, with its sophisticated technology and weaponry, we still hear of something called "friendly fire"—when rockets, missiles and bombs attack and kill one's own troops or allies in war-zones.

What a needless and tragic waste of human lives!

Nations today, are plunged in the darkness of ignorance and believe that they can assert their sovereignty and integrity only by waging war against their enemies. Worse, they actually believe that lasting peace can be established through relentless war. Thus, our world is scarred by violence and strife. But when the darkness of ignorance is dispelled by the first glimmer of understanding, we will realize that different races and different nations are members of one global family. How grievously will we then repent our misdeeds! Piteous is the need of the nations for such a light – the light of oneness, the light of brotherhood, understanding and compassion.

It was the nuclear bomb which brought the Second World War to an end—but at what cost? Hiroshima and Nagasaki are horrendous reminders that nuclear devices cannot bring about peace by wholesale destruction. In fact, nations have woken up to the fact that they cannot have such a thing as military 'victory' when it is sure to be followed by mutual annihilation! What are the world's leading statesmen doing about this frightening possibility?

Nevil Shute's powerful novel *On The Beach* portrays the last surviving human beings to be left alive after

Australia—and perhaps the entire world—has been devastated by a nuclear explosion. Its deadly radiation reaches a remote seaside town in Australia after every other place on earth has been left as a ghost-land. The loneliness, the horror and the misery of the last few survivors on earth are told in the novel with spine-chilling realism.

It is said that m y developed countries have built ultra modern, high-tech 'nuclear shelters' at the cost of millions of dollars of public money. I am told that these underground bunkers can actually withstand nuclear explosion and radiation—and each one can accommodate about fifty or hundred people.

What about the rest of the country? What about the rest of the world? What about the rest of humanity?

How can anyone build a bomb shelter and feel 'safe' about it? How can we spend vast sums of money on 'defense' expenditure, acquiring weapons of mass destruction and feel 'secure' with it? A little common sense would tell us that preparing ourselves for a nuclear war simply means preparing for the elimination of the human race—including ourselves. In the words of John F. Kennedy, "Mankind must put an end to war, or war will put an end to mankind."

Hundreds of thousands of people in the world today do not have nutritious food to eat, clean water to drink, or even fresh air to breathe. One does not have to be a financial analyst to know that if the nations of the world stop spending astronomical sums in designing, manufacturing, procuring and acquiring destructive weapons, these basic necessities can be made available to all people of the earth!

Let me narrate to you a story which I read recently. An extraterrestrial being—ET for short—comes to our earth to try to understand earthlings. Having landed in an isolated spot, he sets out, in human form, to explore the world of men.

On the first day, he comes across a military camp. At a secluded corner of the camp, he finds four young soldiers engaged in bayonet practice. The ET can't understand what's going on, and asks the young men to explain it to him. The young men tell him about the bayonet—a sharp knife attached to the barrel of a rifle—and how it can be used to kill enemies at close quarters. They also show him straw dummies on which they learn to thrust their bayonets in such a way that ensures killing.

Horrified by this barbaric exercise, the ET asks the young soldiers, "Do you enjoy this kind of exercise? Do you actually like killing people?"

"Of course we don't," the young men tell him. "But we have no choice in the matter, and we have to obey the command of our authorities."

The ET moves on. Later that day he comes across a crowd of cheering people who have gathered at a public square. Peeping over their shoulders, he sees a young man in uniform, being decorated with a medal.

"Why is he being honored thus?" the ET asks a bystander.

"He is one of our national heroes," the man tells the ET. "Single handedly, he killed fifty men in a battle, and brought victory to our country."

The ET looks at the young man with horror. He seemed to be barely 25 years old, and he had killed 50 men single handedly!

That evening, sitting on a park bench, the ET hears an announcement on the radio, that a man has been sentenced to death and would be executed the following week.

"Why is this man to be put to death?" the ET enquires of the people listening to the broadcast.

"He killed two men," they answer, with grave faces.

Returning to his spacecraft, the ET thinks things over, and wrote in his journal: "Here on planet earth, young men are taught to kill people with efficiency and accuracy. Those who kill a large number of men are rewarded with medals. Less efficient killers who kill only a few men are punished with execution."

Shaking his head sadly, the ET adds a postscript, "It looks as if mankind is well on its way towards self-extermination".

Doesn't this story make you think about the future of mankind? Doesn't it make you wish that we could move away from the path of annihilation and turn towards peace? When shall we give peace a chance? For believe me, the decision is ours to make. What shall we choose—war or peace?

People and nations, politicians and governments take it for granted that money must be spent on wars. Millions of dollars are spent on arms procurement. Even ordinary people, average citizens, rich and not so rich, are willing to give money for, 'the defense of the country'. We are willing to pay the price for war—but are we ready to pay the price for peace?

The answer is NO! We expect peace to be handed over to us on a platter—for *free*.

We will get peace only when we are willing to pay the right price—and the price for peace is recognition of the higher laws of nature and life; recognition of the ideals of tolerance, brotherhood, understanding and equality.

Here is what some of the bravest generals and commanders say about war. These are men who devoted their lives to fighting for their countries—they faced the enemy frontline, and saw their men die in the battle. They were men who led from the front.

General Oman Bradley said: "Wars can be *prevented* just as surely as they can be *provoked*, and we who fail to prevent them must share in the guilt for the dead."

General Douglas Mac Arthur said: "I have known war as few men now living know it. Its very destructiveness on both friend and foe has rendered it useless as a means of settling international disputes.

How can wars settle disputes? How can wars bring about peace? Peace can be brought about only by a change of heart, a change of attitude among men.

The greatest need of humanity today is peace. The tortured, wounded soul of humanity has cried piteously for peace, age after age. World fellowship and world unity—in these two simple ideals is the panacea for all the social, political evils that afflict humanity. The world belongs neither to you nor to me! We are here as pilgrims on earth. Our stay here is but for a little while. The world belongs to God—He is our President. Under His sovereign rule we must establish a world union in which every nation lives as the brother of every other nation.

I recall an incident in the life of Gautama the Buddha. One day, the Enlightened One learns that two armies, owing allegiance to two rulers are ranged on either side of the river Rohini. Both are ready to attack, to annihilate each other—all for the sake of the waters of the river. The issue at stake is: Which kingdom has greater rights over the river?

The Buddha comes before them. Addressing the two kings, he says to them, "Tell me, O, kings! How much is this water—the water flowing in the river—worth?"

The kings bows down before the Buddha, for they revere him. "Lord, water is worth very little," they answer as one.

"How much are kings worth?" the Buddha asks.

"Oh, kings are worth a lot. Their value is inestimable, immeasurable," comes the reply.

"And how much are your people worth?

"Our people are worth everything to us—we fight to protect them, for they are very precious to us."

"Are not these soldiers your people?"

"Each of them is as precious to us as our own children!"

"You say water is worth very little – and yet you are prepared to shed the blood of these soldiers whom you claim are dear to you as your own sons! Why are you bent on destroying your lives and the lives of your soldiers? You are ready to fight over a river: Will you let flow a river of blood for the sake of the river water?"

The words of the Enlightened One go into the very hearts of the kings. They promise that they will make peace with each other.

I recall these beautiful words from the Old Testament:
And they shall beat their swords into plowshares,
And their spears into pruning hooks;
Nation shall not lift up sword against nation,
Neither shall they learn war any more.
But they shall sit every man under his vine and
under his fig tree;
And none shall make them afraid;
For the mouth of the Lord of hosts has spoken.

—Isaiah Ch. II, verse 4

If we want peace, we must be prepared to pay the price for peace! If we want universal peace, we must create a new humanity.

I am not a scholar or an analyst. I am a simple pilgrim, a wanderer, a vagrant of the Lord who keeps moving from place to place, moving wherever the Lord takes me, moving in quest of fellow pilgrims in whose hearts there may be a deep hunger for peace.

And the more I have thought of it, the more it seems to me that there are three things that are needed to create conditions for an enduring world peace. The first is the spirit of brotherhood, the spirit of fellowship. The second is the spirit of service. And the third is a new vision of life as a movement onward.

The Spirit of Universal Brotherhood

Every morning in Indian schools, children recite the prayer of unity which begins thus:

India is my country. All Indians are my brothers and sisters.

I love my country and I am proud of its rich and varied heritage.

I shall always strive to be worthy of it.

I shall give my parents, teachers and all elders respect and treat everyone with courtesy.

To my country and my people, I pledge my devotion.

In their well-being and prosperity alone lies my happiness.

Considering the fact that we are now beginning to call our world a 'global village,' I think it is also time we modify this prayer thus:

The world is my family, and all human beings are my brothers and sisters.

I love my world and I am proud of its rich and varied heritage.

I shall always strive to be worthy of it. I shall give my parents, teachers and all human beings respect and treat everyone with courtesy.

To my world, my country and my fellow human beings, I pledge my devotion.

In their well—being and prosperity alone lies my happiness.

Does this not sound beautiful?

May I say to you, this is not a revolutionary new idea that I am expressing! Our ancient *rishis* spoke thousands of years ago about the concept of *vasudaiva kutumbakam*— the world as one family. The Tamil Sangam poets of the 3rd Century AD sang, "Every place is my home; everyone is my relative!" No other world scripture expresses the spirit of universal brotherhood as beautifully as the *Vedas:*

> *Om sarvesham swastir bhavatu*
> *Sarvesham saantir bhavatu*
> *Sarvesham poornam bhavatu*
> *Sarvesham mangalam bhavatu*

> Auspiciousness be unto all,
> Perfect peace be unto all,
> Fullness be unto all,
> Prosperity be unto all.

> *Sarve bhavantu sukhinaha,*
> *Sarve santu niramayah*
> *Sarve bhadrani pasyantu*
> *Maa kaschid dhukha bhag bhavet*

Happiness be unto all,
Perfect health be unto all,
May all see good in everyone
May all be free from suffering.

What a wonderful, universal prayer this is!

Sadhu Vaswani often said, "Children of the earth, ye all are one."

I am told that there is a magnificent archaeological site in Western Africa – the vast ruins of Jenne in Mali. Apparently, this was a city of over 100,000 people one thousand years ago. It was, in fact, a world class metropolis in the first millennium, far surpassing London in size and importance.

A visitor to the site observes: "Its art was stunning. Its architecture reflected a complex society . . . What struck me most, however, was the fact that it had been completely ignored by western archeologists for decades, because they found no evidence of military constructions! The Jenne civilization did not find its strength through military conquest or intimidation of its people, but through cooperation! It was a great city built not on fear, but friendship!"

Mary Baker Eddy, the founder of the distinguished newspaper, *The Christian Science Monitor* wrote of her vision of the brotherhood of humanity in 1908:

For many years I have prayed daily that there be no more war, no more barbarous slaughter of our fellow human beings; prayed that all the people of the earth . . . love God supremely, and love their neighbors as themselves.

If mankind was created by God, is not our brotherhood an established fact?

David G Stratman narrates a moving story—a real-life story—about the First World War in his book, *We CAN Change The World.* It tells us about a Christmas in 1914 in the trenches of Europe. The captains and generals had taken 'time off' for Christmas, and only the common soldiers on both sides were left to guard the battle lines on both sides.

On Dec. 25, in a spontaneous move, British, French and German soldiers dared to disobey their superiors and fraternize with the 'enemy.' German troops actually held up Christmas trees from the trenches with the signs which said, "Merry Christmas", and "You no shoot—we no shoot." French and British troops responded eagerly to the move, and hundreds of soldiers on both sides crossed the 'no man's land,' to sing Christmas carols, exchange greetings and show photographs of loved ones back home. Men shared rations, played football and even roasted food over camp fires for a common meal.

When the high command of both sides heard about this, a collective shudder ran down their spine. They could not—would not allow it! If soldiers asserted their brotherhood, how could wars ever be fought?

Generals on both sides declared the spontaneous peacemaking to be treasonous, and soldiers who participated were subjected to court martial. By March 1915, the budding brotherhood movement was systematically crushed—and the killing machine put back in full operation.

Armistice was declared in 1918—by then fifteen million soldiers had been killed.

Not many people have ever heard of the Christmas truce of 1914. The story was systematically suppressed by authorities on both sides!

This story goes against the popular conception of war and 'enemy' nations. But it shows us that the world can be a different place if we set our hearts to it!

I firmly believe that until we grow in this vision of brotherhood, world peace can never be a reality. "May we grow in the spirit of fellowship and understanding," say our ancient Hindu scriptures. And the *Rig Veda*, perhaps the oldest of all scriptures says: "Together walk ye, and together talk ye, and together know ye your minds!"

The world, I believe is a garden of God. God is in all that is—men and women, birds and animals, fish and fowl, worms and insects, in trees and flowers, in rivers and rocks, in stones and stars, in this pen that scribbles, and even the paper on which my moving finger writes, "Krishna! Krishna." Krishna is in all—and we all are in Krishna! When we have this vision of the One-in-all and All-in-one, we will grow in the spirit of Brotherhood of all creation!

One day, I was out on a walk with a few of my friends. A man brushed past us, walking in a hurry. Our eyes met only for a second, and I folded my hands in greeting. The man was under such stress that he continued on his way without a response.

One of my friends said to me, "Dada, you greeted him with a *namaste* and he did not even return your greeting!"

My reply was, "I fold my hands only to pay obeisance to the God who resides within everyone, and not to greet the outer form!"

Is not this the vision of the One-in-all, given to us in the Vedas? Sri Krishna tells us the same thing in His song Divine, the *Bhagavad Gita:*

> Who sees Me
> Deathlessly dwelling
> In all that is,
> And who sees
> All in Me –
> Of him I shall not lose hold
> Nor shall he lose hold of Me!

Our hearts need to be saturated with love, for love is the light which will illumine the world. For this, developed brains are not needed; we need enlightened hearts that can behold the vision of fellowship, unity and brotherhood. Love is what we need to build a new humanity, a new world of brotherhood and peace. We must eliminate the dark forces of greed, selfishness, prejudice and mistrust—and cultivate the power of Love which is the power of Peace!

In this connection, may I share with you the "Fellowship Song" which I penned long ago?

> The whole earth is our country,
> And the sky is its dome;
> The nations are as mansions
> In th' Heavenly Father's Home!

We of Chin' and Japan,
Of 'Merica and Ind,
We all are brothers, sisters –
Of Soviet and Sind!
Hindus, Muslims, Christians, all
Buddhists and Baha'is –
We share each other's friendship,
And the love that never dies!
One is the faith we live by
One is the song we sing!
With little deeds of service,
We worship Him, our King! …
We trust in God, His mercy,
And in ourselves believe!
All that today we hope for
We shall one day achieve!
Hand in hand, we march on still,
A better world to build,
A world of love and laughter,
With peace and plenty filled!

I have always asserted that Hinduism is not a religion, but a way of life. And the Hindu way of life embraces the whole of God's creation in its entirety! For Vedanta teaches us that there is but One Life in all! The One Life sleeps in the mineral and the stone, stirs in the vegetable and plant, dreams in the animal and wakes up in man. Creation is one family so therefore let us not forget, that birds and animals too, are our younger brothers and sisters! It is our duty to guard them and protect them!

My vision of fellowship and brotherhood shows me a world in which the right to life is accorded to every creature that breathes the breath of life! How can wars cease until we stop *all* killing? How can we claim to seek world peace when we continue to slaughter sentient creatures? For if a man kills an animal for food, he will not hesitate in killing a fellow man whom he regards as an enemy! Therefore I urge you, let us grow in the true spirit of brotherhood. Let us grow in the spirit of Reverence for all Life!

The Spirit of Service

The first thing needed for enduring peace among nations is the spirit of brotherhood.

The second important thing we need to create conditions for an enduring world peace is the spirit of service.

The spirit of service! Peace cannot be achieved by politics, power and diplomacy. True peace is possible only through the spirit of service. If I had a million tongues, I would appeal to you with each one of them, especially to my young friends who are going to be tomorrow's leaders and opinion makers—seek not power! Seek service!

Let us do as much good as we can, to as many as we can, in as many ways as we can, on many occasions as we can and as long as we can!

How can the world be peaceful and prosperous if one fraction of its people live in luxury and opulence while the majority live in poverty and deprivation? Therefore, we must all learn to share what we have with others! Let us set apart a portion—say one-tenth—of our earnings to be utilized in the service of God and His suffering creation.

To some of us, who are unable to make two ends meet, or live within their income, this may at first appear a very difficult thing to do! But we will find eventually, that in the measure in which we share what little we have with others, we will be truly blessed—and this world will be a better place for our humble endeavors!

The shortcut to world peace is through love, compassion, the spirit of caring and sharing and service. It is also the shortest and quickest route to God. The way of service is closely allied to the way of brotherhood—for we need to assert, again and again, "I am my brother's keeper!"

And who are our brothers? Our brothers and sisters are all those who suffer and are in need of help—men, women, birds and animals. We must become channels of God's mercy, help and healing, so that His love may flow out to them through us and our actions. When we become instruments of God's love, there is no limit to what we can accomplish. In God's divine plan, we can become the sanctuary of the weary and heavy-laden; we can, with our efforts, become a source of sweet, refreshing waters in the wilderness that is this world.

There is a story in wide circulation about a question asked of Rabbi Hillel—a notable rabbi from the 1st century BC. Someone asked the rabbi to teach him everything about the Torah while standing on one foot. Rabbi Hillel responded: *"What is hateful to you, don't do unto your neighbor. The rest is commentary. Now, go and study."*

There is a simple question that all saints ask of us: How can we claim our love to God if we do not love our fellow human beings? How can we call ourselves human beings if we watch our brothers and sisters suffering and struggling?

God is Absolute Love—and if we love God, we must be imbued with the longing to serve our fellow men. I believe that true service is a spiritual activity, which at its best, is born out of the Love of God. It was a true saint of God who said: Prayer without work is as bad as work without prayer!

God cannot be satisfied with our adoration and devotion if they come only from our lips—for words and alphabets cannot make a prayer. It is our hearts and our own lives that must bear witness to our devotion—and what better way to achieve this than through the service of our fellow human beings?

It is possible that some of you may be really overcome by doubts and anxiety when I talk about service to humanity; you may think to yourself, "After all, we are not millionaires. We are people with limited means at our disposal. How can we aspire to serve suffering humanity?"

God can use the least of us in great acts of service, when He so wills. When Jesus fed the five thousand people who had followed him into the hills, he did not use his chief disciples, the apostles as they were called later. In fact, they were full of tension and anxiety, and planning to send the crowds away. Instead, Jesus turned to a small boy whose mother had packed a simple lunch for him. But this boy was willing to give all he had in perfect trust to the Master. I am sure there were many wealthy people in the crowd who had better food with them, but I doubt if they had the faith, trust and devotion of the little boy, who was willing to give his lunch away when the Lord asked him to.

This is the great gift of service—it blesses him who receives and him who serves!

"What do we live for if not to make the world less difficult for each other?" asks the distinguished writer and novelist, George Eliot. Most of us are inclined to be self centered, and to live narrow, selfish lives—but it is only in selfless living that we can discover the best that we are capable of. And do not restrict 'giving' to the giving of alms, giving money to the poor! You were surely made for higher things—so give of yourself, give of your time, talents and energies to lighten the loads of the weary and the heavy-laden!

Albert Schweitzer was always pained to hear people say, "If only I were rich, I would do great things to help and serve others." He would point out to them that all of us could be *rich* in love and generosity, and that we could always give our loving interest and concern to others— which is worth more than all the money in the world!

Nowadays, we use the word 'philanthropist' to describe a multi-millionaire who donates vast sums of money to charitable organizations. Many of us do not know that *philanthropist* is derived from two Greek words, *philas,* which means loving, and *anthropos,* which is man. In other words, the root meaning of philanthropist is a loving man. Aren't we all capable of becoming philanthropists? Of course we are—if we give of ourselves, from a heart filled with love.

"If you want others to be happy, practice compassion," the Dalai Lama tells us.

In loving and compassionate service, in selfless and caring service lies the secret of a peaceful, united world community.

A woman once wrote to evangelist Billy Graham, saying that her life had become empty after her children had grown up and left home. She was filled with gloom— she felt lonely and useless.

Billy Graham pointed out to her that until then, her immediate family had utilized all her time and energy. Now, it was time for her to further extend the range and scope of her love. He reminded her of children who needed understanding and care in her community; he spoke of old people who needed companionship. "Why don't you get out of your narrow circle and find the joy of helping others?" he asked her.

A few days later, she wrote back to him, "I tried your prescription. It worked! I have walked from night into day!"

Of course charity begins at home, but it need not stay put there! Extend your service to the society, the community in which you live. Let your community reach out to others—and you will find that the whole world is soon linked by the spirit of selfless service!

"Let everyone who comes to you return to their life feeling better and happier," Mother Teresa would often say to her helpers. If we all tried to follow this simple precept, wouldn't we leave the world a better and happier place?

And the ways to do this are numerous. To quote the poet H.W. Longfellow:

No man is so poor as to have nothing worth giving; as well might mountain streamlets say they have nothing to give the sea because they are not rivers! Give what you have. To someone it may be better than you dare to think!

Can you read? Then read to a blind student. Can you write? Then write a letter, fill a form for someone who is not so lucky. If you are not hungry, share your food with someone who is. If you are happy, contented, at peace with yourself, reach out to those who are not as fortunate as you.

We all have something to give! Let us give with love and compassion, and we will make the world a better place!

How can I refrain from quoting those beautiful lines that have never failed to inspire me!

I shall pass through this life but once.
Any good, therefore, that I can do
Or any kindness that I can show to any fellow creature,
Let me do it now.

Let me not defer or neglect it,

For I shall not pass this way again.

Don't hold back! Don't underestimate yourself and your abilities! Don't imagine that you cannot make a difference! We may feel that our effort is but a drop in the ocean—yet every drop counts in the ocean of service!

On an unforgettable day, Sadhu Vaswani and a few of his devotees went walking by the river. It was a beautiful day, and a congenial mood prevailed among us—for I was privileged to be in that blessed fellowship.

All of sudden, a shadow seemed to fall on us. The Master was disturbed; pain and grief were reflected in his normally luminous glance.

We followed the direction of his eyes—and we saw what he had seen. A lone fisherman sat on the bank of the river, catching fish. He had already landed a few fish, which were put into an earthenware pot of water kept beside him.

The Master approached the fisherman and said to him, "Can you sell to me all the fish you have caught this morning?"

The man stared at Sadhu Vaswani, puzzled. To his experienced eyes, this was no average customer for fresh water fish. And anyway, why did he not come to the fish market where he would have a wise choice? And then, why did he want the entire catch of the morning?

"Why do want all my catch?" he asked, guardedly.

"Because," Sadhu Vaswani said, "I would like to release the whole lot into the water."

"And what about my livelihood?" the man demanded.

"I do realize that you must earn your living, my friend," the Master said. "This is why I offer to *buy* the fish from you."

"How much will you offer for this lot?"

"Whatever you ask."

The fisherman decided to argue his case further. "Alright," he said, "Supposing you were to buy this lot from me and release them into the water—what difference will it make? I'm not the only fisherman here; there are hundreds of us. So you release five fish—five small shellfish into the water—what difference will it make?"

"May I show you?" the Master asked him gently.

"Do show me sir," said the man. "I would like to see what difference it makes."

Sadhu Vaswani asked one of us to offer the man twenty rupees – for the Master carried no money with him. The fisherman's eyes widened in surprise, for it was more than the few fish were worth!

"May I?" said Sadhu Vaswani, gently lifting the small pot of water. He poured just a little of the water into the river—and out jumped one little fish. Oh, you should have seen the tiny creature frisk and play in the flowing waters! It seemed to know, instinctively, that it had managed to escape the jaws of death!

The fisherman stared at it—as did all of us. He had seen fish squirm and stiffen as he hauled them up from the river. This reversal of his daily process took his breath away! And the fish seemed to dance and swim merrily before his eyes!

"You see, it makes a great deal of difference to her," the Master said to him.

As he emptied the contents of the pot, five bright and lively fish repeated the joyous performance before our delighted eyes.

"You *can* make a difference," the Master repeated.

Ralph Waldo Emerson urges us to realize that we can leave the world a better place in many simple ways—by producing a healthy child, by creating a clean, green patch of garden, or by a reformed social condition. Even if one person breathes easier because of you, it makes a difference! There is always some work that will never be done if *you* don't do it; someone who would miss *you* if you were gone; somewhere there is a place which *you* alone can fill!

You can make a difference. Let me give you the words of Bertrand Russell:

It may seem to you conceited to suppose that you can do anything important towards improving the lot of mankind. But this is a fallacy. You must believe that you can help bring about a better world. A good society is produced only by good individuals, just as truly as a majority in a presidential election is produced by the votes of single electors.

We regard ourselves as responsible citizens. We pay our taxes and our bills on time; we exercise our franchise and fulfill our democratic duties; we try to obey all traffic rules; we steer clear of breaking the laws of the land; we try not to interfere in other people's affairs . . .

But this is not enough! Doing our duty is alright – but we need to do our duty *and a little more!* The opposite of love is not hate but indifference, or apathy—to the needs of those around you. We need to contribute our share—our mite—to the welfare of the world; to what Sri Krishna called *lokasangrha.*

Little drops of water make the mighty ocean! Little grains of sand make this beautiful land. So too, when we all perform little acts of service, little deeds of kindness, the world will be a better place.

Let us turn for inspiration to St. Francis's prayer:

Lord, make me an instrument of thy Peace,
Where there is hatred let me sow love
Where there is injury, pardon;
Where there is discord, let me bring truth,
Where there is doubt, faith;
Where there is despair, let me bring hope
Where there are shadows, may I bring thy Light;
Where there is sadness, let me bring joy.
Lord, grant that I may seek rather to comfort than be comforted;
To understand, than be understood;
To love, than be loved;
For it is by giving that one receives,

It is by forgetting self, that one finds,
It is by forgiving, that one is forgiven
It is by dying that one awakens to eternal life.

A New Vision of Life

We all want peace—peace of mind, peace in the family, peace in the community around us, peace between countries, peace in the world, peace with our environment. As I said, there is scarcely a soul upon the earth that does not yearn for peace. But how many of us are prepared to pay the price?

I will tell you what I think is the price we must pay: We must love one another. I will go one step further: We must love one another or perish!

We must love each other; we must pray for each other; we must be prepared to sacrifice for each other; we must put aside selfishness and narrow national interests and work for the goal of world unity.

Once I happened to talk to an expert technician, who had worked as a welder for years together. He explained to me that welding was possible only when the materials to be welded were brought together at the temperature of *white* heat – which, as all of you know, is far above the *red* heat we normally talk about. If the temperature is not that of white heat, you simply cannot weld materials together. Even if one of the materials to be welded is not at white heat, welding cannot be done. All objects to be welded have to be at white heat.

So it is with world peace. Lasting peace cannot be achieved unless all of us, working together, striving together, generate the white heat of idealism, determination and resolution which will lead us on to peace.

I believe this white heat can be generated by the third dimension I spoke to you about—the third essential condition to achieve world peace, which is *a new vision of life as a movement onward*. For we need to have a vision, we need to dream dreams to work towards the achievement of this ideal.

What do I mean by a new vision of life as a movement onward? Let me explain.

I believe a new age is dawning, a new cycle in history which has started. The nations, races and peoples of the world must unite together to march onward, forward, Godward!

Godward, I say. For God and religion cannot, must not be kept out of this vision. Religion must not be set aside, even though people tend to discredit religion these days. As for me I repeat my firm belief that it is not religion that has failed us, it is we who have failed religion. It is we who have failed religion, because we only speak of religion, we do not bear witness to it in deeds of daily living. We do not bear witness to the teachings of the great prophets. It is life that is needed, not words! I may recite prayers, chant hymns and sing songs of praise, I may read unending passages from the scriptures, I may go to the Temple, the Church or the Mosque seven days a week—but if I do not bear witness to the great ideals of my religion in d   ; of daily living, am I any better than a gramophone or a tape recorder? I may even write wonderful commentaries on the *Bhagavad Gita*, the *Upanishads* or any other world scriptures, but if I do not reflect the teachings of these scriptures in my actions and words, am I better than a desktop printer?

The world does not need gramophones, tape recorders or printing machines. True life is needed; true religion is needed in terms of vitality, energy, life. "Blessed are the peacemakers," said Jesus. The world today needs peacemakers—not those who merely talk of peace, but those who carry peace within their hearts and transmit it to those around them. It is people such as these who can save the world, which, today, is madly rushing from danger to destruction. Blessed are the peacemakers. May they heed the words of Jesus, "Be not hearers of the Word, be doers of the Word." They will be the saviors of our sinking civilization!

Our leaders and statesmen have dreamt of such a vision. A few years ago, they set up what is known as MDG—Millennium Development Goals—common to all people, all nations so that together, the world could take on the political, economic, cultural and social challenges that are facing us today.

The MDG represents something like a checklist of development, with nations taking on the task of reducing poverty, establishing universal primary education, reducing infant mortality, reversing the spread of epidemic diseases etc. There were other universal objectives like promoting gender equality, sustaining the environment and developing international partnership.

When these 'development goals' were first made known, many rich countries saw them as targets meant of other, less developed countries beyond their shores. They felt that they had already achieved most of these goals—and it was best to leave these goals for 'others'.

This was six or seven years ago. Since then, there has been a profound change in the world – especially in the attitude of the richer countries. This impact came in a drastic way—from terrorist attacks, natural disasters, unforeseen climatic changes, terrifying new virus infections, bewildering technological changes and rapid economic fluctuations.

The Sultan of Brunei, addressing the UN on the MDG, made a significant observation: That the expression, "the world beyond our shores" has ceased to have any real meaning in today's context. In geographical terms, there may be countries across the oceans, beyond our shores, he observed; but the reality is that there is just one world which we all share. And the future of the planet will involve all the countries, developing more and more contact with the rest of the world. His Majesty reiterated, "We will be more and more affected by what happens outside our borders—and we will be more and more dependent on that outside world."

You might ask: What has this got to do with my onward vision? It is this: That our future peace, prosperity and security depend not only on ourselves or on our own nation, but the success and well-being of all the nations!

No matter what our backgrounds, cultures, beliefs, faiths and histories, we are involved in the future of the world together. Unless everyone achieves the desired goals, there can be no lasting peace and security. Every missed opportunity, every failed goal would be a root cause of global insecurity.

When we achieve the goal of universal peace, as well as the more specific developmental goals, we would be eliminating the 20th century concept of 'first', 'second' and 'third' world countries. There will be just a single 21st century world in which all of us will have shared hopes and shared responsibilities.

One World; one vision. This is the hope that sustains enlightened thinkers and progressive organizations. It is not just a dream any more—it has already become an economic and commercial reality with the WTO opening up boundaries, and once secluded nations like China and Russia emerging from behind the Iron Curtain to enter into economic collaboration with the rest of us.

But this cannot stop at just the commercial levels. We have to move onward, forward. After all, we share one world; we live on the same planet. Is it not our responsibility to make this world a better place to live in, for ourselves and our children, and our generations unborn?

One is the world—and the only one we have. Isn't it time we took care of it and its resources? And shouldn't we begin by taking care of one another? How can we take care of one another if we are constantly quarrelling, constantly bickering and waging wars with one another?

It was a very wise soul who said, "The world can only be as good as the people in it." So let us resolve to be good—to get better, so that this world can benefit with our efforts.

True, we need to change, we need to develop; we need to make progress. But the change must be for the better—not for the worse. The progress and development must be for everybody's benefit, not for the privileged few alone.

The daunting problems of violence and strife in our world have to be tackled on a war-footing —if I may use such a contrary metaphor! The need for achieving world peace is fundamental. No extrinsic attempts to achieve it are likely to be crowned with success. The pity of it is that all our plans and schemes till now consider only the political and economic aspects of the problem, and ignore its spiritual dimensions. And it is my humble opinion that politics and economics, unaided by spiritual ethics, only cause confusion worse confounded.

The outer is always an expression of the inner, and world peace cannot be achieved unless we have first established unity in the hearts of men. Politics, after all, sweeps only on the surface of life, and cannot touch men's hearts. On the other hand, religion goes to the very root, and transforms the lives of individuals, their thinking, their morals, their conduct and character. Politics is the product of the mind and the intellect—and these are often instruments of division. True religion is born of intuition and higher understanding—and these are essentially unitive. This is why I affirm that we need a new unitive vision of the spirit. We must turn our attention from the machines and money to the *soul* of humanity.

The great historian Toynbee, surveying the situation of civilization in the twentieth century, pointed out that the world's hope is not in love of money and power, but in the spiritual qualities of justice, tolerance, sympathy and self-offering to the Eternal.

In the past, religions too, stood impeached at the Bar of Eternal Justice. For the pages of world history are stained with the blood of innocents who have been mercilessly slaughtered in the name of one religion or another. Fanatical crusades drained Europe of men and money, without really improving her civilization. In our own time, we have seen rivers of blood flowing in India and Ireland, Indonesia and Iraq due to sectarian strife and violence.

But is it religion that is to be blamed? Or is it that our lives lack the true religious spirit—which is the spirit of sympathy and service, of peace and fellowship? I think we lack religion in its truest sense. If the great religions of the world could be reconciled and their cumulative powers harnessed to the task of harmonizing different races and nationalities, world peace would indeed become a reality.

Sadhu Vaswani taught me that the various creeds and religions of humanity are but different ways of attaining one goal. Different religions are but branches of one religion—the Religion of the Spirit. No matter how widely they may differ in their externals, they are all born out of one common and universal spiritual need—the need to unite the entire world in a spiritual brotherhood of man. For this is the vision that should inspire us; the vision that will move us onward, forward, Godward!

The Seven Musical Notes of Peace

Western philosophers and thinkers actually believed that when the divine bodies—stars and planets, sun and moon—were at their appropriate locations, their impact on the world, on worldly affairs and on the life of the nations and men would be wholly benign, and good things would happen to the earth. During such benign phases of the planets, they believed that celestial music would issue from the outer reaches of the universe—the music of the spheres, as it was called. This music represented the divine harmony that was brought about, when God created the universe out of primeval chaos. Before God's act of creation, darkness and disharmony prevailed. Out of this chaos and disharmony, God created harmony— the order and beauty of creation. The celestial music of this harmony still resonates in the universe; though, as Shakespeare puts it so memorably:

While this muddy vesture of decay
Doth grossly close it in
We cannot hear it.

That is, in the human form while our soul is still trapped in the muddy vesture of the body, we cannot hear this divine harmony.

What a beautifully imagined metaphor! Everywhere in God's good universe, peace prevails and the divine harmony of peace is played out as celestial music—but human beings trapped in their worldly affairs cannot hear it!

Without peace, life becomes full of discord, disharmony, strife, tempest, tumult. For peace is the true, abiding music of life. I believe that if we so wish, we can create peace on earth through our own efforts.

Even as the musical scale has seven notes, so too the musical scale of peace has seven notes. These seven qualities must be cultivated if we are to have the harmony of peace upon earth. What are these seven qualities? What are the seven notes on the musical scale of peace?

Let us hear the sweet symphony, note by note!

The First Note: Love

Peace is harmony; peace is the music of life. Without peace, the world is lost in a tumult of discord, disharmony and strife. Peace is the music of life—and even as there are seven notes on the musical scale, so too, there are seven notes on the musical scale of peace – seven qualities that we must cultivate if we are to have peace.

The very first note on the musical scale of peace is Love. We must love all—not merely our family and friends, our kith and kin—we must love all creation.

We must cultivate the fine art of friendship; we must make friends with all for the permanent peace plan can only be a friendship plan. Therefore, we must go out and make friends with people belonging to different religions, different communities and nationalities. This is what friendship is all about; not just sticking to the people you know, your neighbors, your colleagues, the people you grew up with.

Let me ask you a question: When you go out for a walk, do you smile at the people whom you meet on the way? Some people will smile back at you; some people will not return your smile, but you have not lost anything! You may win new friends with your smile—and that's what the world needs: Bridges of friendship between people, communities and nations.

Each one of us can become ambassadors of peace, harbingers of peace, merely by smiling the smile of friendship. We can become smile millionaires if we keep on smiling, smiling, smiling.

Sometimes, when I am addressing audiences in different cities, I am struck by the fact that everybody appears to be so serious, so earnest, that they forget to smile! Some of them are even busy taking down notes of the points I make—but they seem unaware of their neighbors, the people seated right next to them.

I stop then and there, and request everyone: "Please turn to either side and smile at those who are sitting beside you." You have to see the visible difference it makes in the auditorium! Suddenly, a crowd of solemn strangers turns into a happy group of friends! The relaxation, the release of tension is so palpable! I have heard it said that a meeting was so tense that you could cut the tension with a knife. Well, when people smile at each other, the waves of friendship that arise can almost be felt, lapping gently around you, easing out all the tension!

Alas, we seem to have forgotten how to smile! Someone said to me the other day that constant frowning actually causes wrinkles on the face, but even that doesn't stop some people from frowning!

On the bus, on the train, on the elevator, in the supermarket, at the lunch counter—smile at the people standing before you, behind you and next to you. You will have made at least four friends and paved the way to peace! So it is that George Eliot tells us: "What sunshine is to flowers, smiles are to humanity. They are *but trifles*, but when scattered along life's pathway, the good they do is inconceivable!"

I often say to myself that the day on which I have not made a new friend is a lost day indeed! When all the people of the world become friends with each other, there will be no wars!

There is an anonymous verse which tells us how we can make friends:

> I went out to find a friend,
> But did not find one there:
> I went out to *be* a friend,
> And friends were everywhere!

Let us then set out to *be* friends, rather than find friends. When we set out to be friends we will find friends—and we will find that friendship blooms in our life.

I hope you would have noticed that I'm not talking about your personal friends, but about a larger concept of friendship with all.

"Friendship with all?" one of you might object. "Isn't that a bit impractical? A friend is someone who has proved himself to you—tried and tested in the trials of life. How can we cultivate friendship with everyone and anyone?"

The first note on the musical scale of peace is LOVE— love as in the Commandment: *Thou shalt love thy neighbor as thyself.* It is this spirit of love that is expressed in the universal bond of friendship. If we pick and choose and reject, universal friendship does not have a chance! As Mother Teresa puts it, "If you judge people, you have no time to love them."

Friendship is a very special kind of love. Love, someone said, may not make the world go round, but it certainly makes the ride worthwhile! This is why former President of the US, Woodrow Wilson remarked, "Friendship is the only cement that will hold the world together."

It is said that true love is rare, even rarer to find is true friendship. To love and be loved is surely the greatest joy of existence! And as Mahatma Gandhi puts it, "It is easy enough to be friendly to one's friends. But to befriend the one who regards himself as your enemy is the quintessence of true religion. The rest is mere business."

This is indeed friendship at its best—not to be friendly with someone who can do you good, but to offer a hand of friendship to your enemies—to love those who hate you!

This incident happened very recently. In a powerful, military nation, hundreds of young men *refused* to perform their military duties in "occupied territories." They were dubbed 'refuseniks' and attacked for their lack of patriotism. But they made a public proclamation about why they took this painful decision. They were all men who had fought to save the country from enemy aggression—but they could not participate in any exercise "in order to dominate, expel, starve or humiliate an entire people."

Make no mistake about this: To an Indian, "Love thy neighbor" means loving the people of Pakistan; to an Israeli, "Love thy neighbor" means loving the Palestinians; to Christians, it means loving the Muslims and Hindus and Sikhs!

Let me remind you therefore, of the words of the apostles:

Bless them that curse you, and pray for your enemies. Fast on behalf of those that prosecute you; for what thanks is there if you love them that love you? ... Do ye love them that hate you, and ye will not have an enemy!

Can we, as human beings do this?

If we could, we are asserting the Divinity in us—and we are helping to spread God's peace in the world!

I repeat, the permanent peace plan can only be a friendship plan. Making friends is a win-win proposition. When we make friends with all, the world will be at peace. Make friends with everyone; even your enemies. Extend your friendship and understanding even to those who are out to commit violence—and you are sure to find that they have hearts receptive to love. Go out to meet them, make an effort to understand them. Don't be afraid of them; don't avoid them or fight with them.

For the permanent peace plan, can only be a friendship plan.

In this connection, can I offer you a practical suggestion? It is a very simple suggestion. Everyday, breathe out this simple prayer at least five times:

May all living beings be happy, full of peace and bliss; may those that are in the north and those that are in the south, may those that are in the east and those that are in the west, those that are tall, those that are tiny, those that are rich, those that are poor, those that are young, those that are old, those that are educated, those that are illiterate, those that are born, those that are yet in the womb unborn, may all, all be happy and full of peace and bliss.

Offer this prayer once on getting up, once before you take breakfast, once before you take lunch, once before dinner, and once before you retire for the night.

Let us go a step further:

May those that love me and those who, for some reason or the other, are unable to love me, may they all be happy, full of peace and bliss. May those that speak well of me, and those that, for some reason or the other, are unable to speak well of me, may they all be happy, full of peace and bliss. May all be happy! May all be at peace!

Let the whole world vibrate with your radiations of peace—and you will bring about peace on earth. The more you radiate peace, the more you pave the way for peace!

Love your friends *and* love your enemies. I look forward to the day—may that day come soon in the life of everyone of you—when you can honestly say, "We have no enemies! All are our friends!"

The Second Note: Equality

Equality! The word has a rhetorical, political and social resonance! Since the French revolution, equality has inspired mankind as a universal ideal.

'Equality' signifies a correspondence between a group of different people or objects. Equality is *not* similarity or familiarity. Thus, when we say, "All men are equal," we do not mean that they are identical or similar. Equality transcends similarity.

Philosophers will argue that the notion of 'complete' or 'absolute' equality is self-contradictory; for the concept of equality presumes a difference between the things under consideration. If things do not differ, they are merely identical.

Equality then, assumes a difference; it teaches all of us to remember our common humanity despite all the differences of class, race, creed, color and religion. It reminds us of Sadhu Vaswani's clarion call: *Children of the earth, Ye all are one!*

Until the eighteenth century, so historians tell us, it was assumed that human beings are unequal by nature. The new ideas generated by the Age of Enlightenment stimulated great modern social movements and revolutions, and the immortal ideals of the French Revolution —Liberty, Equality and Fraternity—captured the imagination of mankind. Needless to say, the principle of equal dignity and respect is now accepted by all right-thinking people.

The Universal Declaration of Human Rights, which was passed by the UN in 1948, was directly inspired by the ideals of the French Revolution. In this crucial document, the concept of human rights was extended to include economic and social rights.

As with so many issues humanity faces, *on paper equality is assured to all of us.* Alas, ground realities are different from constitutionally granted rights and privileges.

Look around you and what do you see? Unequal treatment is meted out to women, the girl child, the economically and socially deprived classes, and to racial and religious minorities. In George Orwell's classic novel of satire *Animal Farm,* we read the dictum that referred to inequality amongst humans: "All animals are equal, but some are more equal than others!"

But equality can begin with us, as individuals. We don't have to interpret laws; we don't have to refer to the constitution. We can meet every human being we come across with the same respect. He may belong to a different creed or class or religion—but we must accord him the same respect that we would accord to any other human being!

In Bernard Shaw's *Pygmalion* , the hero asserts that to him all women are alike—and that he would treat a duchess and a common flower girl exactly alike. The heroine, who is a flower girl tells him that there is a crucial difference between him and his friend, a courteous and chivalrous colonel: The colonel treats even a common flower girl like a duchess; while the professor treats even a duchess like a flower girl. This is not the kind of equality we must cultivate!

It was the German philosopher Goethe who said: "Treat a man as he is and he will remain as he is. Treat a man as he can be and should be—and he will become as he can be and should be."

Shakespeare's Prince Hamlet goes one step further: He rejects the idea of treating people according to their 'just desserts.' He asks sharply, "Treat a man as he deserves—and who shall escape whipping?" Therefore, treat them according to *your* desserts."

The respect and dignity you accord to another should not depend on *his* status, *his* bank balance or *his* position or the size of *his* car and *his* bungalow: rather, it should be determined by *your* dignity and *your* sense of justice as a human being.

There was a time when we lost this sense of dignity and justice—and this led to the shameful practice of slavery.

The French writer and thinker Voltaire rues the fact many men, leaders, and rulers are born with a violent tendency for domination, wealth and pleasure; this is made worse by a strong taste for idleness. Consequently, he argues, men covet the money, land and property belonging to other men—and this leads to subjugation and inequality.

From 1950 to 1990, the world witnessed a protracted period of civil unrest and popular rebellion, when people in several parts of the globe rose together against inequality and social injustice. This process of moving towards equality under the law was a long and painful process in countries like South Africa. In Northern Ireland, Catholics felt that they were denied equal rights; in Africa, blacks felt unequal under white regimes; even in American, the world's richest and most 'liberal' country, blacks demanded civil rights that were denied to them.

The issue of women's equality also had to be fought for. While political equality—the right to vote—was accorded to women in the early twentieth century, economic equality was not so easy to achieve.

In India, Mahatma Gandhi was a seasonal crusader for women's equality. Under his leadership, women emerged from restriction to play leading roles in India's independence struggle. Gandhi never considered women to be unfit for any position or task. "To call women sex symbols is a libel," he wrote. "It is man's injustice to women." He also campaigned for women to become equal participants in family and social life. "The wife is not the husband's slave, but his companion, his helpmate and his equal partner in all his joys and sorrows," he asserted. "She is as free as the husband to choose her own path."

When I talk about Gandhi's respect for women, how could I fail to mention the quiet revolution brought about by my Master and mentor, Sadhu Vaswani? In the days before the term "women's rights" was even coined, Sadhu Vaswani offered the purdah-clad, kitchen-bound women of Sind, *spiritual liberation* in the true sense of the term. His *Sakhi Satsang* (spiritual fellowship of sisters) enabled many women to become decision-makers for the first time in their personal lives—by the very act of voluntarily joining his *satsang*. It would be no exaggeration to say that he inducted Sindhi women into what had, until then, been the domain of men—the practice of religion in the truest sense.

He did everything he could do to break the shackles of superstition and hidebound 'customs' that had kept Sindhi women restricted and confined for centuries. He spoke out against the *purdah* and the evil system of dowry.

His *Sakhi Satsang* was quite revolutionary in its spiritual, moral, social, cultural and economic impact on Sindhi women, if one were to consider the movement in all its aspects. Above all, he emphasized the spiritual *shakti* of women, exclaiming aloud to the male-dominated society, "The woman soul will lead us, upward!"

I concur with Sadhu Vaswani's view that the future belongs to women. We live in a man—made civilization and therefore, men are regarded as superior to women. But a new civilization will dawn—a woman-made civilization, based on the womanly ideals of simplicity, sympathy, service and sacrifice. I believe it is women who will have the *shakti* to rebuild the shattered world in the strength of their intuition, purity and the spirit of silent sacrifice. It is my firm belief that there is a new world in the making—the world of peace, harmony and unity— and of this world the builder would be the woman, not man!

In our ancient Sanskrit language, the word for compassion, *daya,* is feminine—and it has no male equivalent! So it is that compassion is a special manifestation of the woman soul. Incidentally, the Sanskrit terms of women are *abhala* (weak), as well as *mahila* (great)! Personally, I hold no truck with the term 'weaker sex'. I believe women are blessed with great spiritual strength.

I read an ancient Greek story about a city that was threatened by an awful mythical monster, the Unicorn. The warriors and other brave men of the city could not stand up to fight the monster; they fled in disarray. But a pure, simple, young maid confronted the monster—and it was the monster that had to flee from the *shakti* she represented!

I find this story deeply symbolic. For our world today is threatened by the nameless, faceless monster that is compounded of hatred, violence, insensitivity, ruthlessness and strife. It is only the woman—pure, gentle, strong in the spirit of simplicity, service and sacrifice, who can take on the monster and conquer him with her spiritual *shakti*. The woman soul can bring about peace on this troubled planet.

The Third Note: Tolerance

Tolerance, I would say is a highly under-rated virtue! While we elevate love, charity and compassion to the status of saintly qualities, we do not appreciate the more basic and fundamental virtue of tolerance without which peace is just not possible.

The Oxford Dictionary defines the verb *tolerate* as follows: "allow the existence or occurrence of something without authoritative interference; to leave something unmolested; to endure something with forbearance."

Tolerance is, in other words, the practice of allowing of differences in religious opinion without discrimination.

The truth may be one—but the ways to truth are many. You walk along one way—your neighbor, your friend, countless other strangers, may choose a different way. Allow them their freedom of choice!

So many religions are so many ways to the One Reality which is God! God is One; we don't have separate Gods—a Hindu God, a Muslim God, a Christian God and so on. God is One and all the religions are ways that lead to the One. Let each of us follow the path that suits us best.

Live and let live! This is tolerance at its best. Why should I force my neighbor to think and work and speak and worship as I do? Let me accept that all of us are different—and let me respect the difference. For all our differences, for all our diversity in language, culture and religion, we share but *one* world. Therefore, let us accept differences—nay, celebrate all differences, and take delight in them! In difference is variety, the spice of life. In diversity is strength.

In India, we celebrate the plurality and multiplicity of our languages and cultures. The poet Subramanya Bharati described Mother India as the glorious lady who spoke eighteen different languages and had 30 million different faces to show. My friends, that was nearly a hundred years ago. Our population was then just thirty million, and the British recognized only eighteen Indian languages. Today, we are a nation of a billion people, and experts say our people speak over two hundred dialects!

A friend brought me a learned author's book on anthropology. The writer had stated his firm opinion that a race, or a people *without* a common language, a common religion and culture could not call itself a civilization!

I would like to tell the learned writer that he is mistaken. There are homogeneous cultures in the world—and I respect them. But heterogeneous cultures are the contemporary reality in the world today, and we in India have been a pluralistic, multilingual, multi-faith society for over two millennia!

About fifteen years ago, I had the opportunity to address the World Parliament of Religions in Chicago. We were about 3,500 delegates representing religions from A to Z—Anglicanism to Zoroastrianism. I would like to share with you if I may, part of my address to the World Parliament of Religions:

India has always stood up for harmony, understanding and tolerance. Today, India may be passing through a difficult period: but this is only a temporary, transitional phase. The history of India bears ample testimony to the fact that through the centuries, the truth and message of religious tolerance and religious harmony have influenced Hindu people, Hindu society, Hindu political thought, and Hindu state policy—both of large empires and small States—all over India. Unroll the pages of the past and you will find that among all the nations of the earth, India alone has greeted and welcomed with love and respect every foreign religion that entered the country. Judaism, Christianity, Islam, Zoroastrianism, Baha'ism have all become naturalized in India, have become religions of India and have been influenced by the Indian environment. When they first entered India they were all received with respect and love. This is the outstanding example of history.

If this is not a great civilization, if this does not represent the great culture of tolerance and mutual respect, then I don't know what people understand by civilization and culture!

India has become the land of many religions, and Indians have respected every religion. When the great emperor Asoka took to Buddhism, he did not persecute the Hindu majority population in his empire—nor did the people resent his new faith! Even earlier, Mahavira and Buddha, both princes, took to dissenting faiths and views—and the people accepted them and assimilated their teachings. For India has profoundly believed, through the centuries, that God is One, but the ways to reach Him are many. This is why the Hindus not merely tolerate—but accept every religion, praying in the mosques of the Muslim, worshipping in the monasteries of the Buddhists, kneeling before the cross of the Christians, and bowing before the Fire of the Zoroastrians!

Today, you may point out to me that India faces fights and feuds in the name of religion. But I believe that religion came to unite, to reconcile, to create harmony among us. If we quarrel in the name of religion, let us not blame religion for our aberrations: it is not religion which has failed us. It is we who have failed religion!

Prejudice, insensitivity and bigotry can poison the best cultures, if we are not careful. Therefore we must practice, tolerance—the sterling virtue that teaches us to respect people who are different from us.

'Tolerance' seems pale in comparison to 'Love' or 'Compassion'. Therefore, the Reverend Dr. Martin Luther King Jr. used the Greek term *agape*—a sense of universal love that "discovers the neighbor in every man it meets."

In its Declaration on the Principles of Tolerance, UNESCO offers a definition of tolerance which I find beautiful:

Tolerance is respect, acceptance and appreciation of the rich diversity of our world's cultures, our forms of expression and ways of being human. Tolerance is harmony in difference.

May I quote here, the words of Rabbi Menachem Mendel:

Intolerance lies at the core of evil. Not the intolerance that results from any threat or danger. But intolerance of another being who dares to exist. Intolerance without cause. It is so deep within us, because every human being secretly desires the entire universe to himself. Our only way out is to learn compassion without cause. To care for each other simply because that 'other' exists.

Harmony in difference! This is what the world needs today. We need to think, feel and act in such a way, that we contribute to our own sense of inner peace, and also pave the way of peace among nations. For this, we need to respect all those who are unlike us.

The Fourth Note: Mutual Respect between Nations

When patriotism becomes fanatical and narrow, it is called jingoism. When nationalism becomes closed and restrictive, it degenerates into annoyance and hegemony. In a world that talks of superpowers and domination, let me say to you: What we need for lasting peace is mutual respect among people, mutual respect between nations.

"All men are born free and equal," writes the great American poet Robert Frost. "They are free at least in their right to be different."

We fail to treat people with respect when we assume a position of superiority and sit in judgment upon them. And as a wise soul remarks, if nobody seems to 'measure up' to your standard of judgment, it is time you checked your own yardstick!

"No man is an island," wrote the 17th century metaphysical poet John Donne. No man can stand alone—for human survival *inter*dependence, mutual dependence, is the vital law of life. How can we hold our head high when we hold another down? Let us therefore, try and lift others up—and we will find we rise with them!

One Chinese general put it this way:

If the world is to be brought to order, my nation must first be changed. If my nation is to be changed, my hometown must be made over. If my hometown is to be reordered, my family must first be set right. If my family is to be regenerated, I myself must first be!

Respect others—therefore, do not judge others harshly. The trouble with most of us, as Leo Tolstoy points out, is that everyone wants to change humanity while nobody thinks of changing himself! And if we cannot change one's own thinking, how can one change reality?

Vijayalakshmi Pandit tells us of the time when she was head of the Indian Delegation to the United Nations, and had to handle India's complaint regarding the treatment of the people of Indian origin in the then apartheid regime of South Africa. Harsh words were used by both sides. The White South African officials used derogatory language to make personal attacks against India's prestige—and also against Mrs. Pandit.

Extremely agitated, Mrs. Pandit at first retaliated with the same sharp weapons. One day, after a particularly nasty and heated duel of words, she was suddenly reminded of Mahatma Gandhi whom she had known, loved and revered all her life.

Would Gandhi approve of what we are doing, she asked herself. In all his hard-fought struggles against the British Empire, never ever had Gandhi offered hatred or disrespect to the colonizers. The best among the British colonial authorities d also respected the Mahatma. Their fight was pure on principles.

Mrs. Pandit did not want to win the debate through questionable tactics, personal attacks and a vindictive spirit that would ruin her own self-respect. Deliberately, consciously, she made a decision to *raise* the level of the debate—to lift it to the plane of diplomacy where it belonged. Let the White South Africans attack her personally; she would not hit out to them to score a cheap point. Though her opponents at first continued their hate campaign, they were forced to abandon their aggressive tactics and rise to the new high level that she had set for the debate.

Weeks later, when the debate was finally over, Mrs. Pandit crossed the floor to meet the leader of the opposing delegation. She held out her hand to him and said, simply, "I have come to ask you to forgive me if I have hurt you by any word or action in this debate."

Needless to say, her gesture was much appreciated!

Our own self-respect must lead us on to respect others. As Mrs. Pandit observes, "It is good to feel right with others, but even *better* to feel right with oneself."

To retain a sense of proportion, to maintain a proper perspective on life, it is important to respect others.

As we go to the press with this book, the nuclear watchdog bodies of the world have predicted that we are moving even closer to a nuclear war—for in recent years, many nations have joined the once exclusive nuclear club, by exploding their own atomic devices. To compound the problem, there are also 'rogue' traders and experts who are willing to sell missile technology to and build bombs for any nation—at a price.

None of these nations, none of these people would do what they are doing if they had respect for human life!

As I said to you earlier, we all may be different, but we have just this one world to live in. Some of us are extroverts; some of us work very well in teams; some of us get on very well with others. But the fact of the matter is that we all need one another! We cannot live like islands, cut off from the rest of humanity. Therefore we must learn to respect others and live and work amicably with them. Civility is as essential among nations as it is among people!

A memorable experience for me in recent times was my visit to the land of my birth—Sind— which is now in Pakistan. For over fifty years several of my friends had not had the opportunity to go back to the land of our forefathers. Thanks to the new climate of trust and cooperation between India and Pakistan, meaningful dialogues and exchange of visits have taken place between the two countries now. It was this new environment of trust and mutual respect that enabled me to accept a kind invitation from my *Alma Mater*, D. J. Sindh College, Karachi, and 'cross the border' that had divided our two countries in 1947.

Many people were 'concerned' for the safety of our group. They gave me dire warnings about the climate of hatred across the border.

Reality proved to be very different! Our visit to Pakistan was memorable, in every sense of the word. Above all, we were overwhelmed by the love, kindness and courtesy extended to us by the generous people of a neighboring country with whom we have been at war almost constantly!

My visit showed us a new face of the thorny India–Pakistan relationship—the face of thousands of Indians and Pakistanis who had mutual respect for each other and believed sincerely that their future lay in cooperation, not confrontation.

Respect for each other opened wide the door of friendship between the two countries, making people-to-people contact a reality for the first time in fifty years.

I would like to share with you a poem that I composed on that occasion:

> Tear down the walls: we all are one!
> We cannot live apart!
> God is one and the earth is one:
> One is the eternal heart!
> We may discover nature's secrets
> We may plumb the depths of the sea;
> We cannot atone for all the walls
> Which separate you from me!
> Tear down the walls in the name of Allah
> Who is Rehman. Who is Rahim:
> The Master's call has gone forth:
> Work together as in a team!
> Ye all are one!

Ye all are one!
Ye all are one!
Ye all are one!

We extended a hand of loving friendship and respect across the border—and they responded in kindness!

If truth be told, the walls and fences we erect in our minds are perhaps far more formidable than exterior walls and boundaries. The political and emotional 'divide' among the people must be bridged by mutual respect, love and understanding.

There is no power greater than giving respect—alas, we use it so sparingly!

The Fifth Note: An End to Racial Discrimination

How can we ever hope to have world peace when any one race regards itself as superior to another? Therefore, we must put an end to all forms of racial discrimination.

Harmonious integration of pluralistic, multicultural, multiracial societies can only be achieved through good relations based on racial equality.

The notorious 'apartheid' regime of South Africa denied racial equality to blacks and 'colored' people. The word *apartheid*, literally meaning 'apartness' in the Afrikaans language, was a terrible system of racial segregation that was enforced in the Republic of South Africa from 1948 to 1984. Even before 1948, South Africa, which had long been ruled by whites, was racist in its policies and practices. Apartheid was designed to give legal sanction for continued economic and political dominance by people of European descent, while denying basic rights to native South Africans.

We in India, cannot talk of apartheid in South Africa without recalling Mahatma Gandhi's memorable role in the early days of this cruel system. Of course, apartheid had not been institutionalized at that time, but the evil spirit of inequality and racial discrimination had been rampant in South Africa, ever since the Boer occupation.

When Gandhi arrived in Durban, South Africa, in 1893 to serve as legal counsel to the merchant Dada Abdulla, he was asked to undertake a trip to Pretoria. This journey took Gandhi to Pietermaritzburg—an unknown railway station. Gandhi purchased a first-class ticket and took his seat in the first-class compartment. He did not realize that as a non-white, he was not allowed to travel in the first class.

Very soon, the railway officials ordered Gandhi to move to the van compartment, where 'coolies' and non-whites were supposed to take their seats. When Gandhi protested that he had purchased a first-class ticket, he was forcibly removed from the train, and his luggage was tossed out on to the platform.

"It was winter," Gandhi wrote in his autobiography, "And the cold was extremely bitter. My overcoat was in my luggage, but I did not dare to ask for it lest I should be insulted again, so I sat and shivered."

This event prompted Gandhi to take a stand against "the deep disease of color prejudice." In South Africa—and subsequently, in India—as history recalls.

In a just end to the tale of Gandhi's humiliation at Pietermaritzburg Railway Station, in 1997, Nelson Mandela, the President of South Africa, righted a century-old wrong when he conferred the Freedom of Pietermaritzburg on Mahatma Gandhi. President Mandela recalled "Gandhi's magnificent example of personal sacrifice and dedication in the face of oppression."

If you visit Pietermaritzburg today, you will be delighted to see a bronze statue of Gandhi which stands in Church Street, in the city center!

Today, the word *apartheid*, thankfully, is politically defunct. The apartheid regime has been rejected by the world community at large, and by native South Africans, and the transition to a democratic republic, with power devolving to the black majority, has been achieved in a remarkably smooth manner.

If I am talking about the horrors of apartheid now, it is only to remind ourselves that we must not let racial discrimination ever enter our personal, social or professional lives.

Under apartheid, people were legally classified according to their racial groups—white, black or colored—i.e. of mixed descent. They were geographically and forcibly separated from each other. The black majority were herded into 'homelands' not of their choice. Black people were offered *inferior* education, medical care and other public services. A separate Amenities Act actually created segregated beaches, buses, hospitals, schools and universities. Blacks were not even part of the common voters' roll—they had a separate voters' roll. Racial discrimination in work and employment was legalized. If a black man was employed in a city and had the 'pass' to live there, his wife and children were denied the right to live with him! They were confined to non-white areas. These black townships often had no plumbing or electricity. Blacks had to travel in separate buses, which had separate stops. On trains, they were not allowed to travel by first or second class.

The apartheid regime was condemned internationally as racist and unjust. Apartheid was declared as a crime against humanity.

After peaceful protests failed to have any effect, black Africans took to armed resistance and acts of sabotage, and South Africa passed through troubled times. Brutal police and military action became the order of the day.

I would like to draw your attention to one fact: As the majority of blacks were excluded from service in the army and police, all white males had to be conscripted for national service. Unwilling to fight racist battles, many white males actually fled from South Africa.

Internal violence, international condemnation and changing demographic conditions finally brought about the winds of change. Reforms were gradually introduced—and a five year state of emergency lasted from 1985 to1990. On February 11, 1990, Nelson Mandela, the black African leader walked out of prison, after 27 years of incarceration.

The legal apartments of apartheid were abolished, but massacres continued across the country, even as a new constitution was being negotiated. On April 27, 1994, freedom finally came to South Africa's blacks.

In 1993, Nelson Mandela and F.W. de Clerk were awarded the Nobel Prize for Peace for bringing to an end the hated apartheid regime.

The lessons of apartheid must always serve as a warning to mankind—that inequalities and discrimination perpetrated by force will only work towards the detriment of all people! South Africa is still struggling to remove economic inequality and empower its black people.

It was in Durban, South Africa, over a century ago, that Mahatma Gandhi began his historic struggle against racism and inequality. And today in India, we are following Gandhiji's inspiration to wipe out our own evil of casteism—discrimination in the name of caste. This ideological discrimination of an entire community must also be stopped, if India is to enter an era of social and political harmony.

Racism, casteism, and all related practices must be condemned for the evils they perpetrate —discrimination against people founded on false notions of superiority and inferiority; discrimination on the grounds of descent, ethnicity, color or physical characteristics; violent expressions of hostility, hate and bias; perpetuation of social injustice and inequality leading to intergenerational inequality.

I have always said that hate cannot be conquered by hate; so too discrimination can only be wiped out if each one of us fosters tolerance, love and understanding at home and at the work place.

Here is a declaration that a friend sent to me from Tolerance.org, an award-winning website that promotes tolerance, equality and non-discrimination. It is a pledge that each of us must take:

I, (Your Name) will:

- *Examine my own biases and work to overcome them.*
- *Set a positive example of non-discriminatory practices for my family and friends.*
- *Work for equality and understanding in my own community.*
- *Speak out against hate, injustice and all forms of discrimination.*

The world's richest country and most powerful democracy, the United States has also had the specter of racial discrimination casting its shadow on politics and society.

In the 1950's, in America, the equality of all men envisioned in the *Declaration of Independence* was far from a reality. Blacks, Hispanics, and Asians were discriminated against in many ways—openly and covertly. The 50s were a turbulent period in the history of America —and the blacks rose to fight for a new Civil Rights Movement.

Martin Luther King Jr. was the driving force behind the movement. On August 28, 1963, he led a huge rally in Washington D.C. and on the steps of the Lincoln Memorial, delivered a famous speech that has gone down in history as the "I have a dream" speech. Let me quote from this unforgettable oration:

This is no time to engage in the luxury of cooling off, or to take the tranquilizing drug of gradualism. Now is the time to make real, the promise of democracy. Now is the time to rise from the dark, desolate valley of segregation to the sunlit path of racial justice. Now is the time to lift our nation from the quick sands of racial injustice to the solid rock of brotherhood. Now is the time to make justice a reality for all God's children...

I say to you today, my friends, even though we face the difficulties of today and tomorrow, I still have a dream...

I have a dream that one day this nation will rise up and live out the true meaning of its creed: "We hold these truths to be self-evident: That all men are created equal."...

I have a dream that my children will one day live in a nation where they will not be judged by the color of their skin—but by the content of their character...

I have a dream ...

Let us dream of a world where we will realize that all races were created by God—all races belong to God—and that there is no superior or inferior race!

In my secular vision of life, black and brown, yellow and white are the colors of the one beautiful rainbow that we call Humanity.

In my spiritual vision of life, there is no segregation—only Oneness and equality of all human beings, as children of God.

The Sixth Note: An End to All Forms of Exploitation

To exploit another, is to take unfair advantage of him or her. 'Exploitation' acquired a political overtone in Marxist ideology, but it has always had its own moral and ethical significance in human discourse.

Several forms, several modes, several degrees of exploitation exist in our world today. Let us consider a few examples:

1) Non-governmental organizations (NGOs) and service organizations claim that pharmaceutical companies are 'exploiting' cancer patients, cardiac patients and even AIDS victims by keeping the prices of drugs and life-saving medicines artificially high.

2) Developing countries claim that their emigrant laborers and domestic workers are being 'exploited' in rich Middle East countries.

3) It has been reported that Tsunami survivors are being 'exploited' by unscrupulous medical practitioners to sell their organs such as kidneys for a low price—against all laws.

4) It is said that very young children, women, and even prisoners are 'exploited' as laborers in the manufacture of products like matches and fireworks which are potentially harmful to health.

5) Animal welfare activists are opposed to zoos and circuses where, they feel, dumb and defenseless creatures are 'exploited'.

6) Typically, Marxism has always claimed that the capitalists 'exploit' the working classes through low wages, harsh policies, and unsatisfactory working environments.

Exploitation is the utilization of something or someone's services in an unjust, cruel or selfish manner for one's own advantages. If a transaction is mutually advantageous, it ceases to be exploitative.

In social and economic terms, exploitation involves a transaction in which a group of people are persistently and unfairly mistreated for the benefit of others. Thus, slavery was one of the worst forms of human exploitation.

In ethical terms, exploitation involves the treatment of human beings as mere 'objects' or as merely a means to serve others' ends. People are regarded as *resources* for utilization without any consideration for their welfare or well-being.

In today's context, developing countries are the focus of much controversy over the problem of exploitation—particularly because of the global economy. It is said that multinationals pay workers in these countries very low wages, as compared to those that prevail in their home countries. This is a form of corporate exploitation.

We also hear of 'sweatshops'—unsafe, overcrowded premises where workers are really shut up and forced to work long hours. Obviously in such cases, unequal human standards are adopted in developing and developed countries.

Child labor is one of the worst forms of exploitation. It refers to the employment of underage children as part of a regular work force. This happens in factories, quarries, agriculture, hotels, small businesses, and restaurants. We are now beginning to hear also of children being forced to join military outfits. This is something all of us should be ashamed of!

I am of the firm opinion that all our transactions, all our relationships, should be based strictly on the principle of justice. For exploitation, in the long run, leads only to hatred and conflict.

Animal abuse is   another form of exploitation. This involves cruelty to animals, and causing them unnecessary harm and suffering. Personally, I feel that factory farming and even animal testing are barbaric practices, unworthy of any evolved civilization. For me, cruelty to animals is a *moral* issue.

There are people to speak up against all other forms of exploitation, and you will forgive me if I voice my support for the dumb and defenseless creatures. They have no press, no TV, no media, no spokesperson to voice their grievances. They need friends, they need spokespersons!

Have you ever spared a thought for the atrocities that are perpetrated on the animals day after day, in laboratories and in slaughterhouses? Have you thought of these creatures imprisoned in their tiny cages, deprived of light, fresh air and free movement, compelled to stand and live in their own filth? Have you thought of animals 'stunned' and then hung upside down in a line to have their throats slit? And after this appalling treatment, they are finally eaten up—consumed! And this nightmare goes on, day after day.

My friends, let me tell you, there will be no peace on earth until we stop the exploitation of animals—until we stop all killing! All killing must be stopped for the simple reason that if man kills an animal for food, he will not hesitate to kill a fellow human being whom he regards as an enemy.

Current civilization, built as it is on the exploitation of the poor, and on the blood of the dumb, defenseless creatures, is crumbling beneath the burden of its own weight. The new civilization that is to dawn, must be built on a nobler, worthier ideal. If civilization is to endure, it must be built in a new spirit of reverence, in a new religion of reverence for all life.

Animal welfare is not enough! We must speak of animal rights! Men have their rights; have animals no rights? I believe the time has come when all animal lovers must get together and formulate a charter of animal rights— a charter of man's duty towards the animal kingdom. I hope and pray that India—the country of the Buddha, Mahavira, and Sadhu Vaswani—will be among the first nations to pass on enactment giving rights to animals.

Every animal has its fundamental rights. And the very first right of every animal is the right to *live!* We cannot take away that which we cannot give! And since we cannot give life to a dead creature, we have no right to take away the life of a living one!

The time is come when we must decide once and for all that all types of exploitation must cease. We must recognize the moral inviolability of individual rights— both human and nonhuman. Just as black people don't exist as resources for white people, just as poor don't exist as resources for rich, just as women don't exist as resources for men, even so animals don't exist as resources for human beings! In the words of my Revered Master, Sadhu Vaswani, "No nation can be free, until its animals are free!"

The world cannot be at peace until all forms of exploitation cease!

The Seventh Note: Compassion

A friend shared a beautiful definition of compassion with me. It comes from the Internet encyclopedia, wikipedia.org:

> Compassion is a sense of *shared* suffering, most often combined with a desire to *alleviate* the suffering, to show special *kindness* to those who suffer. Thus compassion is essentially *empathy*, but with an *active* slant in indicating that the compassionate person will actually seek to aid those they feel for.

I would describe compassion as the crown of all virtues. I believe it is this quality that takes us closest to the Divine within each one of us. When we practice—not just feel—compassion, when we go out of ourselves to reach out to others and alleviate their suffering, we rise to the Highest Self in us. Need I say that at such times, negative feelings of strife and disharmony are totally nullified in our hearts and minds? And when more and more of us practice the divine quality of compassion, will our world not move towards lasting peace?

All religions, all cultures exalt compassion. Hindus see the Goddess Lakshmi as the very personification of *Daya*. The Lord is referred to as *Dayallu*, and compassion for humanity is His chief attribute.

There is a beautiful story told to us in the *Brihadaranyaka Upanishad:*

In the beginning of Creation, Prajapati's (the Creator's) children—gods, men and demons—completed a period of penance and appealed to the Lord for His counsel.

First, the gods (*devas*) approached Him and said, "Please instruct us."

The Creator gave them a single syllable—"Da." He asked them, "Have you understood?"

The gods said, "Ye, we have understood. You have said *dama*—you tell us to control ourselves."

Next, the men said to Him, "Please instruct us. To them, God gave the single syllable, "Da" again.

"We have understood," they said. "You have said *daana*—you tell us to Give."

The demons came up with the same request, and God uttered the same syllable, "Da."

"Yes, we have understood," the demons told Him. "You have said *daya*—you tell us to have compassion."

"Da, Da, Da," is repeated through the heavenly voice of thunder—"*Dama, Daana, Daya.*" *Control yourselves; give; have compassion.*

The poet T. S. Eliot was so touched by this extract, that he actually uses this episode, inclusive of the Sanskrit terms in his masterpiece, *The Waste Land.* According to the poet, "Da, Da, Da" is the solution to all the problems and spiritual ills that afflict modern civilization.

When we talk of compassion, can service be left far behind?

My Master, Sadhu Vaswani, put it in admirable words: "Service of the poor is worship of God."

Is not service the best form of worship? And is not compassion the very root, the fountainhead of service?

The concept of compassion is also central to Buddhism. For human beings are afflicted with various kinds of *dukha* or sufferings, associated with old age, sickness, death, grief, pain and despair—and the spirit of compassion is what we require to wipe out human suffering to the best extent possible.

Christianity, too, regards compassion as a blessed quality. "Blessed are the merciful," Jesus said. "For they stall obtain mercy."

Islamic scholars tell us that compassion is central to Islam — in fact, it represents the true spirit of Islam. Allah's own names *Rahman* and *Rahim* (The

Compassionate, the Merciful) are the names by which every devout Muslim invokes Allah in his daily prayers.

Dear friends, *talking* about compassion is not what we need today! My purpose in citing these various scriptures is only to show that all major religions of the world lay emphasis on compassion—compassion in thought, word and action!

Many of us are ready to love and sympathize with those who are close to us—relatives, friends, loved ones. We may go out of our way to help them—but when strangers are involved, do we rush to their help, or do we simply turn away? *This* is the true test of compassion.

Some of us are ever willing to help our fellow human beings—but what about animals? How many of us kill animals to nourish our own lives? How can this be reconciled with true compassion?

The greatest form of compassion can only come by understanding the central concept of Vedanta—that all life is one. The life that sleeps in stones and minerals, the life that dreams in plants and trees, the life that stirs in animals and birds is the same life that awakes and breathes in man. And this life is the very spark of the Life Universal.

There is a parable that tells us of a mother with paralyzed arms, who saw her child swept away along the fast moving currents of a river, but was unable to do anything to save the child. This illustrates the fact that *feeling* is not enough—we have to act; we must find the means and ways to relieve others' sufferings and pain— this is *meaningful* compassion.

I am sure Aung San Syuu Kyi needs no introduction to you. This remarkable and courageous woman became the leader of the democratic movement in Burma. Placed under house arrest by the military regime, she was awarded the Nobel Prize for Peace in 1991. Here is what she has to say about compassion in the context of world peace:

> The essential distinction between savages and civilized men lies not in differences of dress, dwelling, food, deportment or possessions—but in the way we treat our fellow human beings. It is the degree of humanity in our relationship with others that decides how far we have traveled from a state of savagery towards an ideal world of civilized beings who truly have learnt the art of peaceful co-existence.

There are many ways of defining humanity. I would like to define it in terms of *bodhi-chitta*—the mind of enlightenment. Those filled with both compassion and wisdom add greatly to the positive civilized forces of the world by combating savage passions that urge men to inflict suffering on their fellow human beings.

Compassion without wisdom is ineffective; wisdom without compassion is soulless. When a compassionate heart is linked to an insightful mind, then we can make a significant contribution to peace upon this earth.

God is all Love. God is all Wisdom. He expects us to live and work not merely for our own pleasure and our own benefit, but also for the service and benefit of others. Is it not more blessed to *give* than to receive?

Compassion does not require a hefty wallet, strong limbs or heroic deeds or great and austere sacrifices.

A helping hand, a friendly word or gesture, a kind smile will more than suffice! And let me add, in the words of Mark Twain: "Kindness is a language which the deaf can hear and the blind can read"!

Compassion binds the world together in the bond of unity and peace. In the words of the Buddha: "In separateness lies the world's great misery, in compassion lies the world's true strength."

May I also quote these beautiful words from the Indian poet saint Tulsidas:

> Compassion is the essence of life:
> Pride takes you to hell.
> Tulsi says: Do not give up compassion.
> Till the last breath leaves the body.

THE THIRD DIMENSION
AT PEACE WITH NATURE

At Peace with Nature

Let me begin my discussion on the third dimension of peace—peace with Nature—with the beautiful opening *shloka* of the *Shanti Sukta* from the *Atharva Veda*:

Om Shanta dhyou
Shanta prithvi
Shantam idam uranthariksham
Shanta udhanvatirapa
Shantana sant aushadi
May peace prevail in the skies
May peace prevail on earth
May peace prevail in vast space
May peace prevail in the flowing river, and in
plants and trees!

Are we at one with the invocation of the rishis? Are we, today, at peace with nature?

No — we are not! I am sad to state that we are in fact at war with nature!

We can see it in the way we treat the soil; we can see it in the way we have destroyed the habitat of wild animals; we can see it in the pollution of our waterways, the degradation of our environment, the depletion of the ozone layer and the complete and utter waste of Mother Nature's resources.

Although I said "Mother Nature," I doubt if we have the right to call ourselves her children anymore! We are actually a vital component of nature, and it is our sacred obligation to preserve and protect this planet that God has given to us as a habitat. Alas, we live upon earth as if there is no tomorrow—as if we care nothing for unborn generations who will continue to live here long after we are gone!

As the crown of God's creation, we should have been guardians, protectors, wardens of Nature. Instead, we have exploited her shamelessly, selfishly—and O, so foolishly.

I am aware that the fashionable, trendy words to use today are 'ecology' or 'environment'. But I chose the word Nature, deliberately, because it is close to my heart. It is a term that is known and loved by millions of men and women worldwide. It is associated with peace, purity, serenity, unspoiled beauty, tranquility and the transcendental spirit of the Universe. It recalls to my mind the *pancha tattwa*, the five elements—earth, water, fire, air and space—of which our Universe is composed. It encompasses these myriad aspects of creation, hundreds of thousands of living beings and organisms, those stunningly beautiful landscapes, mountains, rivers, seas, forests, deserts, mangroves, lakes and plains that man could not have made—but alas, which he seems to be destroying irrationally!

How can the world be at peace, when we are threatened by natural disasters—which are in fact, perpetuated by man's negligence and greed?

I do not need to remind my readers that the last few years have seen catastrophic events hitting the earth one after another. The Tsunami of 2004, the terrible hurricanes and floods of 2005, and the massive earthquakes with which 2006 began—these were deadly years indeed! Let me refer to a fascinating book—*In Defense of Nature: The History Nobody Told You About,* by Richard Michale Pasichnyk:

> The end of 2004 to the beginning of 2006 —a period of a little over 365 days —has been described as one of the deadliest years in the history of modern man. Nearly three hundred thousand people were killed by the Tsunami and the earthquake; over one hundred and fifty seven million people were involved in the disaster, losing their homes, livelihood and loved ones. While the loss of human lives was tragic and overwhelming and invaluable, we paid the price in terms of economic costs too!
>
> Munich Re, one of the world's largest reinsurance agencies, reports the following figures for disaster-related economic losses:
>
> 2003 — $ 65 billion
> 2004 — $ 145 billion

The reason why I'm quoting these figures is not because I put economic losses above human loss, but to bring home to you the enormity of the disaster that we have brought upon ourselves. I am afraid that today, cash costs speak louder than life losses!

When I say that we have brought these disasters upon ourselves, some of my friends protest politely. "This is not our doing," they tell me. "Man is incapable of causing disasters of this magnitude. And then, such natural disasters have occurred since the dawn of creation, starting with the melting of the Ice Age. How can man be held responsible for the unbridled fury of nature?"

With due respect to my friends, I beg to differ.

It seems so easy to view these disasters as "acts of God", as "unfortunate catastrophes," as "unpredictable events caused by unfathomable forces of Nature." But we have to face the question: How far is mankind to be blamed for these disasters?

It is one thing to talk of 'natural disasters'—but Mother Nature cannot be blamed altogether. The *degree* and *level* of destruction are the results of human negligence and human greed and human selfishness.

In his bestselling book *An Inconvenient Truth*, former Vice-president of the United States, Al Gore, writes:

The climate crisis is, indeed, extremely dangerous. In fact it is a true planetary emergency. Two thousand scientists, in a hundred countries, working for more than twenty years in the most elaborate and well-organized scientific collaboration in the history of humankind, have forged an exceptionally strong consensus that all the nations on Earth must work together to solve the crisis of global warming.

The voluminous evidence now strongly suggests that unless we act boldly and quickly to deal with the underl ₃ causes of global warming, our world will ndergo a string of terrible catastrophes, including more and stronger storms like Hurricane Katrina, in both the Atlantic and the Pacific. ...

Consider the following man-made factors which were responsible for the severe losses inflicted by Hurricane Katrina in the U.S:

- Rapid urbanization
- Indiscriminate growth and construction
- Systematic destruction of coastal wetlands
- Loss of valuable coral reefs and other marine phenomena on the Atlantic coast.
- Location of polluting industries like chemical plants, oil—refineries and toxic—waste producing factories in the New Orleans area.

Thus the problem of human actions, human errors cannot be overlooked. Rampant, unsustainable development compounds the effect of natural disasters, making their impact far worse!

May I draw your attention to a significant fact? If you look at the photographs and TV footage of Hurricane Katrina, you can see hundreds of destroyed homes and power lines and collapsed buildings—but trees and bushes are left standing! How would you account for this?

Let us not forget that transgressing the laws of Nature brings these disasters upon us—and if we do not learn from our mistakes, we shall be forced to repent them!

Experts would agree that natural disasters like earthquakes are often in response to an imbalance in the ecosystem, such as a disrupted and disturbed habitat. This is why many of them occur in urban centers, agricultural fields, dams and other structures of 'civilization' which have destroyed natural wilderness.

Let me quote Henry David Thoreau: "In wilderness is the preservation of the world."

We destroy mangroves at our own peril—for it is a known fact that they could have acted to protect the worst effects of the Tsunami on coastlines.

We interfere with coral reefs to our own detriment — while only a handful of people died in Maldives, thousands were killed on the beach resorts of Thailand. Rampant construction was one of the reasons.

Other 'human' factors are unchecked population growth and migration to cities, misguided land use, and global warming.

Construction regulations are non-existent—or they are criminally violated. Inferior construction caused a major loss of lives in the Pakistan earthquake of 2005.

"Indiscriminate economic development and ecologically destructive policies have left us more vulnerable to natural disasters," says the Worldwatch Institute, an environmental group in Washington.

A classic example of this was the monsoon floods that hit Mumbai in August 2005. The commercial capital of India was unceremoniously turned into an ugly version of Venice—the floating city. We now know that it was not only inadequate drainage, but also loss of green areas, the clogging of a lifeline river, and exploding housing schemes on landfill areas that worsened the disaster in human terms.

Such human folly is not exclusive to developed or developing countries—and unfortunate comparisons were made between Hurricane Katrina and the Mumbai floods.

In all these cases, natural disasters were made worse, their impacts compounded by human folly and greed.

Oliver Smith, a distinguished anthropologist says that 2005 may not have been a freak year—but the start of a manmade cycle of disasters. He warns us that our obsession with economic growth must be checked—and people's consciousness must be changed, to face their accountability for these disasters.

We must learn to live at peace with Nature, we must cultivate a symbolic relationship with her—or we will hurtle down the abyss of self-destruction.

Peace with Nature means that we must avoid blatant errors such as:

- Habitat destruction
- Deforestation
- Environmental pollution

- Nuclear tests and explosions
- Indiscriminate Mining

And how can we condone or justify the way we treat animals—our younger brothers and sisters in the one family of creation, whom we are morally obliged to protect!

O the sin of daily slaughter in our cities! How can we have peace on earth until we stop all killing?

And one passing thought to share with you—among all the creatures on earth, only man alone has the capacity to interfere with the ecological balance. Elephants do not destroy forests and uproot trees; tigers and lions do not destroy their own habitats; birds and insects do not pollute the air, anymore than fishes pollute rivers and seas.

It is man's responsibility to protect the environment, preserve the ecological balance. It is his sacred duty to see that the integrity and diversity of Nature is maintained. For to destroy Nature, is to destroy mankind.

According to the Hebrew Scriptures, humans are conceived as superior to all the rest of creation, which exists merely for his use and exploitation. However, according to Midrash —— the method by which the ancient Jewish Rabbis investigated Scripture in order to make it yield laws and teachings that were not apparent in a surface reading —— God is reported as saying to man: *'All that I have created has been for your sake; take care then not to spoil and destroy My world.'* In other words, God put a restraint on man, enjoining him to care for the various orders of creation 'beneath' him. This envisages a hierarchy in creation, with the higher levels expected to exercise responsibility as stewards, guardians and caretakers.

The *Coalition for the Environment and Jewish life* (COEJL) states: "For more than a thousand years Jews have been distant from nature. A reconciliation between Jews and nature is now needed." COEJL member, Rabbi Alexander Schindler, declared:

"The earth we inherited is in danger, the skies and the seas, the forests and the rivers, the soil and the air, are in peril. And with them humankind itself is threatened. As earth's fullness has been our blessing, so its pollution now becomes our curse. As the wonder of nature's integrity has been our delight, so the horror of nature's disintegration now becomes our sorrow."

Every day, in the span of 24 hours, 210 species become extinct—these are rare species of plants, animals and insects. These are living beings which were the products of millions of years of the evolutionary process—and now, they are gone forever. Everyday, hundreds of acres of forests are being destroyed.

And what are we adding to Mother Earth? Everyday, we generate thirteen to fifteen million tones of waste – much of which is non-biodegradable, toxic and carcinogenic. We are exposing our ground water reserves and rivers to all this poison. We are polluting the air we breathe with all these deadly substances.

Alas, we are asleep. When shall we hear the alarm bells ringing? When shall we wake up to the call of our own self destruction?

Reverence for Nature is essential. Reverence for Nature will help us to survive upon this planet. Reverence for nature will help us to preserve and protect this blessed earth for our children—and our children's children.

Reverence is essential—reverence for our rivers and forests; reverence for our lakes and waterfalls; reverence for trees and plants and the grass that grows beneath our feet; reverence for birds and beasts, whom I love to call our younger brothers and sisters.

Sadhu Vaswani spoke to us of the *Prakriti Sangha*— fellowship with nature—which he believed was essential to human happiness. There is a spiritual element in the beauty of nature, for Nature is God's own expression in all its joy. It is the song, the dance of the Lord.

Nature is truly the environment of the *atman*—the eternal soul within each human being.

I remember, I was out on a walk with Sadhu Vaswani, one day—may I say, in the days of my youth, "when I was green in judgment." On the way, a midsize stone lay on the pavement, across our path. Anxious that it should not obstruct the Master's steps, I hastily kicked the stone aside.

Sadhu Vaswani was deeply pained—and I was puzzled. Why should he be hurt that I had put aside a stone? After all, it was only a stone!

I got my answer, in words that I will never ever forget: "If God is in the scripture, is He not in the stone?" the Master said.

God dwells in all nature—therefore let us cultivate reverence for Nature!

III
LOOKING AHEAD

A Meditation on Peace

Peace and happiness go hand in hand. What we imagine to be 'happiness' is often nothing but a momentary, transitory feeling of pleasure. True joy is closely allied to peace. I give you a description of joy and peace from Sharon Salzberg, one of America's leading teachers of meditation:

Alas, for many of us, such moments of peace are too fleeting; if we wish to experience this peace, calm and stillness *within* us, irrespective of what is happening in our lives, we need to cultivate an inner core, an inner centre of peace—deep within us, a centre of peace to which we can retreat whenever we wish, that nothing can disturb and nothing can dispel.

Can I offer you a simple exercise—a meditation on peace? This exercise is so simple and so easy, that you can practice it daily, in sessions of five to ten minutes.

Step 1: Sit in a relaxed posture. As far as possible, the back, the neck and the head should be in a straight line. In the beginning you may find it difficult to bring them all in a straight line, but do it as far as possible. Above all, be relaxed. Relax your body, relax your muscles, relax your limbs. Make sure you are seated comfortably and focused inward.

Step 2: Now visualize a tranquil scene before your mind's eye. It may be the silver waters of the sea on a calm, moonlit night; it may be a majestic mountain peak capped with virgin snow; it may be the dark green, cool and shady interiors of the woods in the springtime; it may be the misty, verdant slopes of a hillside—imagine any scene that has been long held in your mind as a precious memory, or recalled from a picture you may have seen, which fills you with a sense of peace and joy. Close your eyes and picture yourself there, in your favourite location. Feel the peace and tranquillity all around you. Let it enter your heart and soul and permeate every pore of your being.

Step 3: Now take deep rhythmic breaths. Be conscious of every breath you take. As you breathe in, tell yourself that you are inhaling the peace of God, the peace that passeth, surpasseth understanding. As you breathe out, you are exhaling calmness all around. There is peace within you, there is calm all around you. Reflect on this beautiful passage from the Vedas:

May there be peace in the higher regions; may there be peace in the firmament; may the waters flow peacefully; may all the divine powers bring unto us peace. The Supreme Lord is Peace. May we all dwell in peace, peace, peace; and may that peace come into each of us.

You are now in an environment of serenity and peace. You may, if you like, imagine yourself seated on a rock in the midst of an ocean. Waves arise. They dash against the rock. The rock stands still and sturdy, unaffected, calm, tranquil, peaceful, and serene. Waves arise. Waves are the distracting thoughts. They dash against the rock. The rock of your mind is unaffected, calm, tranquil, peaceful, and serene.

You now begin to realize your oneness with all that is, all men, all creatures, all things, all conditions. You are not apart from others. The others and you are parts of the one great whole. You are in every man, in every woman, in every child. You are in every unit of life, in every bird and animal, in every fowl and fish, in every insect, in every shrub, in every plant. You belong to all countries and communities, all races and religions. You are at one with the universe. As you become aware of this oneness of all creation, you find your heart filled with loving kindness and a spirit of kinship and compassion with all things, all beings in this vast and wonderful world.

Step 4: And now we come to the crucial, final stage of this meditation. In this stage, you breathe out peace and happiness, goodwill and bliss to all. May all be happy and full of peace and bliss. Think of all who dwell in the Northern lands and pray in the heart within: "May all who dwell in the Northern lands be happy and full of peace and bliss." Then think of all who dwell in the Southern lands and offer the prayer, "May all who dwell in the Southern lands be happy and full of peace and bliss." Likewise, "May all who dwell in Eastern lands and all who dwell in Western lands, may they all be happy and full of peace and bliss."

Breathe out peace and goodwill to all. May all be happy and full of peace and bliss. All living things whether they be near or far, big or tiny, rich or poor, educated or illiterate, whether they be born or are still in the womb unborn, may all, all, all be happy and full of peace and bliss. May those that love you and those that for some reason or the other are unable to love you, may those that speak well of you, and those that for some reason or the other are unable to speak well of you, may all, all, all, without exception, be happy and full of peace and bliss. You are in them all. It is only when they become happy that you are happy. May all be free from disease, ignorance, and sorrow.

The Final Step: Open your eyes gently and feel peace infusing your body, mind, heart and soul.

As you get up from this meditation, you will find that you yourself are happy and full of peace and bliss!

The Way Ahead

The task that lies ahead of us is breathtaking in its utter simplicity and mind-blowing in its critical significance.

The task is to build a new world—a world without wars, a world without wants, a world in which peace and joy will be every man, woman, and child's birthright. The task is to create peace—or perish. The choice is ours.

The future must belong to a new civilization where man will be a truly evolved super-being, who sees every human being as his equal, his friend, his brother, his sister.

Who will build this brave, new world?
To them, let me say:
Build your own lives first, in peace and non-violence!
To the youth—the inheritors of the earth—I say:

Let there be an unquenchable thirst, and insatiable hunger in your hearts for peace. Let there be a divine unrest in your spirit so that you will not be content with gold and riches, power and position. Let there be a spiritual yearning in your lives, so that the cult of comforts do not make you old before your time.

May you realize the message of Swami Vivekananda and Sadhu Vaswani: That simplicity is strength and all imitation is weakness. May this quality of simplicity flower into service and sacrifice.

The power of our sympathy, simplicity, service, and sacrifice will and then surely build a new civilization, a new world, a divine humanity!

Epilogue

All around us, today, is a ring of darkness. But darkness cannot stay for ever. When I look into the future, it is so bright, it burns my eyes. It is up to each one of us to make this future a reality.

Let each one of us kindle a little light—a little lamp of kindness and courage and compassion. Let us plant the shady tress under which we will not sit. Let us do little acts of kindness. Is not kindness better than knowledge, more important than wisdom?

Let us be a little more kind than necessary. Be kind, for who knows the next person you meet may carry a hurt in his heart. Let us do what little we can to help make the world a better place to live in. The greatest mistake is made by him who does nothing because he can do only a little!

A new age is knocking at our doors.

When shall we let it in?

Printed in the United States
73481LV00004B/112-438

9 781434 303721